The Digital Practices
of African Americans

Steve Jones
General Editor

Vol. 90

The Digital Formations series is part of the Peter Lang Media and Communication list.
Every volume is peer reviewed and meets
the highest quality standards for content and production.

PETER LANG
New York • Washington, D.C./Baltimore • Bern
Frankfurt • Berlin • Brussels • Vienna • Oxford

Roderick Graham

The Digital Practices of African Americans

An Approach to Studying Cultural Change in the Information Society

PETER LANG
New York • Washington, D.C./Baltimore • Bern
Frankfurt • Berlin • Brussels • Vienna • Oxford

Library of Congress Cataloging-in-Publication Data

Graham, Roderick.
The digital practices of African Americans: an approach to studying
cultural change in the information society / Roderick Graham.
pages cm. — (Digital formations; vol. 90)
Includes bibliographical references and index.
1. Information technology—Social aspects—United States.
2. African Americans—Social life and customs. 3. Internet users—
United States. 4. Information society—United States. I. Title.
HN90.I56G73 303.48'3308996073—dc23 2014005851
ISBN 978-1-4331-2272-9 (hardcover)
ISBN 978-1-4331-2271-2 (paperback)
ISBN 978-1-4539-1335-2 (e-book)
ISSN 1526-3169

Bibliographic information published by **Die Deutsche Nationalbibliothek.**
Die Deutsche Nationalbibliothek lists this publication in the "Deutsche
Nationalbibliografie"; detailed bibliographic data is available
on the Internet at http://dnb.d-nb.de/.

© 2014 Peter Lang Publishing, Inc., New York
29 Broadway, 18th floor, New York, NY 10006
www.peterlang.com

Table of Contents

Introduction

The route that brought *The Digital Practices of African Americans: An Approach to Studying Cultural Change in the Information Society* to fruition was not a standard one. It all started with a bit of frustration I experienced while selecting course materials. As with most professors, I teach courses that are general, and fit the needs of the department—Introduction to Sociology, The Family, Urban Sociology, and courses that are related to my specialization—Race and Cyberspace, Internet and Society. In courses that are departmental needs I always found myself referring to the Industrial Revolution in a similar way. I would say: "The Industrial Revolution was a shift in the economy of society. The way in which people produced goods changed dramatically. At the same time, there was an equally dramatic change in the types of technologies available. But, the Industrial Revolution also changed [topic here]." And then I would delve into the social and cultural changes.

In my Sociology of the Family course, I talk about how the growth of factories pulled men away from the home. This created a devaluing of women's work, as cash was not attached to their very important home activities. It also created a separation of the sexes, and helped produce an ideology of separate spheres, where men "should" be in the public sphere of work and politics, and women "should" be in the private sphere of home. In my Urban Sociology course I talk about how the growth of cities was due to the growth of manufacturing. Cities, urban environments we can call them, are not progeny of the Industrial Revolution per se, but like the current growth of cities in Africa, Latin America, and China it intertwined with the growth of manufacturing. With this as a context, I spend time talking about how social life changed in the city, how people who had crammed into cities for work now had to recalibrate their social interactions. In both cases, the Industrial Revolution was about not only economic and technological transformations, but also social and cultural ones.

Meanwhile, when teaching courses in my specialization, I found it harder to use the same spiel for the Digital Revolution. I couldn't refer to literature that explored the social and cultural transformations. Sure, there was literature out there, but it was very thin. More importantly, I couldn't find *sociological literature* that explored the social and cultural effects of information and communication technologies (ICTs) on society. This was odd. It had been 40 years since computing became available to everyday people with the advent of the personal computer, about 20 years since the Internet was readily available and 10 since the mobile phone became easily attainable. However you wanted to label our new age—digital age, computer revolution, network society, or information society—it was clear that things had changed. Yet, sociologists were not producing work that I could use in my classes, and I needed to look in disciplines like communication and law. This literature was of high quality and informative, yet the questions that are asked in these disciplines are not always the same as those asked by sociologists and the answers given do not always coincide with a sociological interpretation of phenomena.

It was the frustration I felt when I juxtaposed the ease in which I could cite sociological research on the social and cultural changes associated with the Industrial Revolution, and my inability to do so for the Digital Revolution that gave me the idea to write this book. I surmised that this lack of literature was not just a problem for classroom instruction. More sociological research on issues related to ICTs could inform civic leaders and policy makers outside academia. I decided that the best way to (somewhat selfishly) have better teaching materials for my classes, and (somewhat more altruistically) address the vacuum in scholarly work was to develop a perspective that could spur future sociological research on ICTs.

The most dominant research on ICTs seemed to suffer from techno-economic determinism. There was a lot of research on the change in the economic structure because of ICTs, and its consequences. There was also a lot said about the technology. But, social and cultural changes were downplayed, or at worst seen as occurring because of changes in the economy or technology. I even saw this techno-economic determinism in the media. Story after story talked about which tech company's stock had risen or how much money they would raise in their initial public offering of stock. When stories about social and cultural trends were mentioned they were trivialized. For example, online dating is often framed as a quirky way to socialize, not a fundamentally new way that intimate relationships are initiated.

I saw this techno-economic determinism as a consequence of the dearth in sociological studies. The lenses through which scholars and society's leaders see the Information Society are focused too narrowly. They can focus on the economy:

- Where will the jobs be in the next 20 years?
- Are our schools preparing us for the new economy?
- What tech companies had the largest initial public stock offerings last year?

The lens can also focus quite well on technology:

- How will Web 3.0 change the user's experiences on the Internet?
- What will the spread of 4G connectivity on mobile phones mean?
- What are the particular characteristics of this mobile application that has made it so popular?

But the lens does less well for generating questions about the construction of racial identity, the reproduction of inequality, the manufacturing of belief systems, and other sociological questions. And so the primary purpose of *The Digital Practices of African Americans: An Approach to Studying Cultural Change in the Information Society* is to construct a new lens through which to view the social and cultural transformations occurring in the Information Society.

But once the project was underway, I realized I had secondary purposes. First, I wanted to make this book accessible to the broadest range of readers possible. I wrote with the undergraduate student in mind, knowing that hitting this target meant more advanced readers would be fine (obviously it doesn't work in the opposite direction). My experience as a teacher of undergraduates has made it clear that students (and most people generally) comprehend abstract ideas more readily when connections are made to instances from everyday life. And so numerous examples are used, including examples from my own life. I try to avoid jargon. When presenting results from empirical studies, jargon is often unavoidable, and indeed is necessary. However, technical terms are explained as much as possible without hindering the flow of the narrative. For those readers who are still unsure of the finer points of the data analysis, skipping these sections will not prevent an understanding of the main ideas. Another decision I made was to profile scholarly work from some of the most influential writers and thinkers. Academic articles tend to hide the individual author, and extract the main ideas. I chose to highlight the work of one or two of the more prominent scholars, to give the reader a sense of who are the more prominent thinkers in the field.

Another secondary purpose was to illustrate the agency that minorities currently have in the Information Society. A deliberate choice was made to use African Americans as illustrations of the digital practice perspective. In later chapters I explain that one of the reasons was because my African American background produced an inherent interest, and my knowledge of African American social and cultural conditions made it easier for me to apply the digital practice perspective to them. The fact is that minorities, and here I am mainly referring to African Americans and Hispanics, are not as disadvantaged vis-à-vis ICTs as one might think. Minorities have become very adept at using technology to overcome structural and historical difficulties, so much so that I cannot imagine labeling them disadvantaged with respect to this domain of life.

Given the very real unequal outcomes for minorities in so many areas of life, and the wealth of scholarly work showing the many digital divides between whites and minorities, I suspect that my view will be unconventional. But, as with everything else in this book, the key is to look past economic and technological aspects, and see how minorities use technology to achieve their goals in everyday life. From this angle minorities are extracting immeasurable benefits. They are finding ways through their own ingenuity and creativity of mitigating racial inequality through ICT usage. Scholars, policy makers, the media, and most importantly minorities themselves, need to be aware of this so that it can be nurtured and the potential of ICTs can be realized.

The plan of the book is as follows. In Chapters 1 and 2 I talk more about the lenses that suffer from techno-economic determinism. In Chapter 1 I discuss the models of the Information Society, focusing on the writings of Daniel Bell, Manuel Castells, and Yochai Benkler. In Chapter 2, I discuss the digital divide metaphor as another lens too narrowly focused on the economy and technology. Because this concept has been appropriated by the mass media and by policy makers, more attention in this chapter is placed on the wider society's usage of the term.

In Chapter 3 I introduce a different way of approaching ICT usage. I explain the two main concepts that make up the digital practice perspective: "digital environment" and "digital practices". The digital environment is defined as the social space produced through interconnected information and communication technologies (ICTs). The digital environment, or DE, is distinct from the physical environment, or PE. It is a space where one must enter via ICTs. Upon entry, one is faced with a new set of social forces, the navigation of which requires adopting new behaviors. Digital practices are the behaviors that result when groups navigate the digital environment.

Chapters 4, 5, and 6 present concrete examples of how the digital practice perspective can be applied. Each chapter presents a case study that explores the digital practices African Americans have developed as they leverage the unique properties of the digital environment. These goals can be keeping in touch with family (Chapter 4), they can be ways to overcome a lack of weak ties (Chapter 5) and they can be the development of an alternative, African American-centered narrative about societal events (Chapter 6). Although the case studies presented here are exclusively on African Americans, the idea is to illustrate how the perspective can be used.

There is a reciprocal relationship between knowledge and social policy. The knowledge we have about the world should inform what government seeks to accomplish and the form that government policies take. Similarly, the issues government deems important—assuming it is representative of the electorate—should inform the types of scientific endeavors undertaken. Since the 1990s, social policy and academic output have been waltzing to the same economic tune. The federal government has been diligent in ensuring that business can grow in the digital environment. In contradistinction, I argue in Chapter 7 that social policy should focus more attention on nurturing nonmarket spaces, and that the digital practice perspective can inform the development and implementation of these policies.

Chapter 8, the conclusion, describes a series of ICT enabled street crimes by minority youth in urban areas called flash robs. These flash robs, I argue, show the potential of ICTs for social and cultural transformation. They are, indeed instances of criminal activity. But they are also examples of how groups in society have leveraged the properties of the DE. It is an example of social and cultural transformation.

CHAPTER ONE

The Information Society

INTRODUCTION

Beginning in the 1970s, information and communication technologies (ICTs) became increasingly important to both large-scale organizations and individual people. These technologies increased our ability to both process information (the microprocessor computer chip, the personal computer) and communicate information (satellites, e-mail, and mobile phones). Scholars have worked to understand the economic and cultural transformations that have coincided with the wide-scale adoption of ICTs. This chapter will review three of these scholars and their theories: Daniel Bell, Manuel Castells, and Yochai Benkler. I will call them models of the Information Society.

While the models reviewed in this chapter are important, I believe that they miss something. The "Information Society", as we currently understand it through these models, is an incomplete picture. There is an overemphasis on economic transformations and technological innovation, and a lack of consideration for social and cultural transformations. The models of the Information Society reviewed in this book illustrate a techno-economic determinism. This techno-economic determinism works on two levels. First, the models can sometimes imply that the co-existing changes in technology and the economy necessarily lead, or predict, changes in culture and politics. This can be seen as a simplistic, first-level determinism. The models I present attempt to avoid this vulgar type of theorizing. Second, the models can imply that the major changes in society are those in the technological and economic spheres. This is a more subtle form of techno-economic determinism. Disproportionate amounts of time are spent detailing the intricate changes in production and consumption, what types of jobs are created, the rise or decline of a given industry, and so. Or, time is spent detailing the new technologies available and what they can do for us. Meanwhile, fairly little intellectual energy is spent on other aspects of society. In this indirect form of determinism, technological and economic changes are seen as necessary preconditions to changes in other areas of society. It is this second level that I think characterizes most scholarly work on the Information Society, including the models I review.

Having pointed out the techno-economic determinism in the Information Society, I will not say however, that these models misinterpret the Information Society. Indeed I think in so many ways they are spot on. The models are not incorrect, *only incomplete*. These models act like so many lenses. They are lenses that deflect our gaze away from social and cultural phenomena and towards technological and economic phenomena. They also distort our view of noneconomic processes associated with ICTs such that while we may notice how much social interaction has changed over the past several decades, these changes are seen as frivolous and insignificant. And so the purpose of this chapter is to summarize some of the more important models of the Information Society and identify some of the ideas that will be used moving forward, all the while keeping the idea in mind that the picture painted by these models is an incomplete one.

MODELS OF THE INFORMATION SOCIETY

Bell's Post-Industrial Society and the Centrality of Theoretical Knowledge

It is appropriate to begin with Daniel Bell (1973), and his text *The Coming of the Post-Industrial Society*. While Bell is not the first, his work has arguably made the biggest mark. Frank Webster (2006), one of the most knowledgeable scholars on Daniel Bell writes:

> "Little social science lasts even a decade, so Daniel Bell's continuing to set the terms for such an important debate is an enviable achievement. It is testament to Bell's powerful imagination and intellect that still now any serious attempt to conceptualise the 'information age' must go back to his The Coming of Post-Industrial Society" (33).

My focus will be primarily on Bell's theoretical approach and core argument. Much has changed since Bell's work in the 1960s and 70s, not least of which is the technology—Bell was writing well before computer networking and personal computing was a norm for everyday citizens. However his theoretical approach and core argument still has meaning today, and has informed much of the theoretical and empirical work that has followed over the last 40 years.

Bell recognized that economic growth in the United States and other Western societies was occurring in the service sector. Already by the 1960s and 70s it had become cheaper to manufacture goods in developing countries, and economic logic necessitated a shift of manufacturing away from the United States. As a result, job growth was occurring in service occupations—occupations that relied on the understanding and manipulating of knowledge—such as education, health, science, and government. It was knowledge and information that powered the economy and produced new wealth, not physical labor.

In order to explain the importance of these trends, Bell developed the "conceptual schema" of the post-industrial society. This schema: "identifies a new axial principle of social organization and defines a common core of problems which societies that become more and more post-industrial must confront" (114). There are, for Bell, three realms that are each ordered by a different set of axial institutions and principles. These three realms are the social structure (the economy and occupational distribution), the political structure (the law making institutions), and the cultural structure (the arena of meanings and symbols).

For all three realms, a major axial principle is the "centrality of theoretical knowledge". Bell argues that economic production, social mobility, and political power derive from the ability to apply abstract theoretical models to the world. An example of such an abstract model would be a computer-generated loss estimate of the number of soldiers that may be lost in a war. Another example would be the mathematical models used to estimate government savings or (losses) from the implementation of a national health care plan. People who can understand, manipulate, and produce these models are those who dominate in the post-industrial society.

Consider the political realm. Beginning in the 1960s political power had been granted to more groups (i.e., minorities in the aftermath of the civil rights movement) at the same time that the reach of government was constantly expanding. The challenge to politicians and their advisors is explaining to the voter decisions about who gets what and why. Similarly, but to a lesser degree, the average citizen must understand how policies affect them. This requires a greater degree of technical knowledge than in previous times:

> "The relationship of technical and political decisions in the next decades will become…one of the most crucial problems of public policy. The politician, and the political public, will have to become increasingly versed in the technical character of policy, aware of the ramified impact of decisions as systems become extended" (364–365).

A few recent political crises in the United States show Daniel Bell to be remarkably prescient. Witness the confusion generated by the American government's response to the Great Recession of the 2008. The highly technical nature of the recession, the deviance that caused the recession (credit default swaps?), and the government's response to it was nearly impossible for people to follow. Most of us were reduced to simply grumbling that people on Wall Street were the "bad guys". Explaining the whole process in TV specials and documentaries became something of a cottage industry.[1] Or, consider the economic rationale behind President Barack Obama's national health care plan. Theoretically, the plan should be an overall benefit economically for the nation. Yet, the administration has had a difficult time explaining its benefits to the electorate, and in turn the electorate has not fully grasped the plan.

For Bell, the post-industrial society can be characterized in this way:

"A…[post-industrial] society is based on services. Hence, it is a game between persons. What counts is not raw muscle power, or energy, but information. The central person is the professional, for he is equipped, by his education and training, to provide the kinds of skill which are increasingly demanded in the post-industrial society" (1973: 127).

Bell argued that the previous industrial age could be seen as a game of man against nature.[2] Man wrestles with the material world to mold it into a form that best suits him. Planes, trains, and automobiles were the results of these battles. Man also fought with his own physical form, as manual strength, endurance, and dexterity were the keys to production. The winners in the game of man against nature were the people, companies, and nations who could invent products sooner, produce them more cheaply, and transport them faster.

However, the post-industrial society is a game between persons. Theoretical models, mathematical formulas, and other symbolic representations are the pieces here. Computer technology is of utmost importance in the post-industrial society because abstract, theoretical models are produced by computer. Bell writes:

"The chain of multiple calculations that can be readily made, the multivariate analyses that keep track of the detailed interactions of many variables, the simultaneous solution of several hundred equations…are only possible with a tool of intellectual *technology* [emphasis in the original], the computer" (1973:30).

The winners in the game between persons are those who can manipulate these symbols. Whereas in the industrial era, the factory owner maintained a superior class position over the worker via his ownership of materials—a Marxian capitalist-proletariat dynamic, in the post-industrial era, class relationships become more complex. The scientist, lawyer, the engineer, the investment banker, and the computer programmer can realistically see themselves on equal footing with owners of property because of their technical knowledge. In this way, the post-industrial economy alters the class structure. As Bell writes:

> "The essential division in modern society today is not between those who own the means of production and an undifferentiated 'proletariat' but the bureaucratic and authority relations between those who have the powers of decision and those who have not, in all kinds of organizations, political, economic, and social" (1973: 119).

Another way to think about the power of theoretical knowledge is to understand its essentially Democratic and meritocratic nature. Increasingly, the people who owned theoretical knowledge were not your captains of industry, who were disproportionately WASPs (White Anglo Saxon Protestant). Bell was writing in the early 1970s when many white ethnics were still discarding their ethnicity and melting into America. Polish, Irish, and Italian immigrants, by this time second and third generation, were steadily moving up the American class structure. They did not have the wealth of WASPs, but used the educational system to attain middle and upper class status.

On the point of the cultural structure in the Information Society, Bell is quiet. Towards the end of his work, he notes that theoretical knowledge presents a serious challenge to the cultural structure, Bell asserts:

> "[There] is a widening disjunction between the social structure (the economy, technology, and occupational system) and the culture (the symbolic expression of meaning), each of which is ruled by a different axial principle. The social structure is rooted in functional rationality and efficiency, the culture in the antinomian justification of the enhancement of the self" (p. 477).

This divergence had been a century in the making, Bell asserts, and had accelerated at the time of his writing. This is an interesting idea—one that Castells will develop with greater detail, and other scholars have pointed out as well (Hassan 2008). However, Bell does not go into much detail about the cultural structure in the post-industrial society.

When assessing Bell's *The Coming of the Post-Industrial Society*, it can be said that while the specifics of his arguments can be critiqued, his main ideas hold true. We are certainly in a knowledge economy today. The trend of manufacturing jobs dwindling, and service jobs increasing has only intensified in the new millennia. One can see Bell's influence in the terms bandied about today to describe people working with theoretical knowledge—"the creative class" and "knowledge workers", for example. Further, theoretical knowledge is now more important than ever before. Political and economic decisions are indeed made by technocrats, who apply data analysis to our most trenchant social problems. A political step is not taken unless polling shows that the step is a feasible one. Decisions on investing are increasingly powered by complex financial forecasts. Gone are the days of "gut" feelings about voters or investments.

But, I believe that Bell's picture of the post-industrial society is certainly incomplete. Despite Bell's comments on the political and cultural realms, his work can be read as ultimately a sociological account of changes in the economy and technology, and *what are the consequences of those changes to society*. And so for about three-quarters of *The Post-Industrial Society* Daniel Bell explains the historical developments leading up to our modern *economy* and how *technology* has aided these developments. With the copious amount of data on the occupational structure, education enrollment, gross domestic product and so on, this is undeniably a treatise on the American *economy*. This is a kind of *techno-economic determinism*.

Bell tries hard to avoid this charge, and his use of axial principles was meant to do the trick:

> "The idea of axial principles and structures is an effort to specify not causation (this can only be done in a theory of empirical relationships) but centrality...it seeks to specify, within a conceptual schema, the *organizing* frame around which the other institutions are draped, or the *energizing* principle that is a primary logic for all the others." (1973:10)

And:

> "In this fashion, one can avoid a single-minded determinism, such as an economic determinism or a technological determinism, in explaining social change, yet single out a primary logic within a given conceptual scheme. One forgoes causality but emphasizes significance..." (1973:12)

Thus, the economy and technology do not, in a single-minded fashion, determine what happens in other areas of society. Are they only more significant? Maybe. But Bell does not show how political and cultural structures influence economic structures. The causal arrow moves from the techno-economic to other dimensions of life. Indeed, Bell writes that political structures can influence economic ones, but he does not develop the idea further. The fact that Bell engages in techno-economic determinism does not invalidate his argument. Instead, it suggests that a more accurate view of the post-industrial society will include a more thorough examination of social and cultural processes.

Manuel Castells and the Space of Flows

Frank Webster writes that Manuel Castells' three-volume *Information Age* "is the most illuminating, imaginative and intellectually rigorous account of the major features and dynamics of the world today" (Webster 2006: 98). In the *Information Age* trilogy, Castells develops a comprehensive theory of information that looks to explain such wide-ranging phenomena as social movements, the growth of women in the workforce, the weakening of the nation-state, and changes in corporate structure. Even more than Bell, Castells' work is far too wide-ranging to cover in a few paragraphs. What follows is not a detailed review of any of the three volumes, but instead major points that I think help develop the overall narrative of this chapter.

Castells begins by exploring the ways in which the economic structure of society has changed, aided by the explosion of computing and communication technology. This change, mirroring Bell's understanding, has had consequences for other spheres of society. For Castells a more fitting appellation for our modern times is "network society", rather than Information Society.[3] This is to emphasize his assertion that what has changed most profoundly in the new age is not the introduction of ICTs as a means of aiding production, but instead the way in which corporations, cities, and people are connected through space and time via ICTs.

Both Bell and Castells believe the origins of the Information Society lie in changes in the economy. Castells argues that in the 1970s the dwindling profits of corporations forced an adoption of new methods of production and a seeking out of new markets. He argues, "The main shift [in the economy] can be characterized as the shift from vertical bureaucracies to the horizontal corporation" (2000: 176). ICTs allowed this horizontal spread to occur because corporations could communicate without regard for space and time: they were "networked". But it was the loss of profits that ultimately forced corporations to make this change.

A major difference between the two theorists is the historical context within which they place this transformation. Castells suggests that the economy of today is not qualitatively different from the industrial economy in sources of productivity and growth. This is in contradistinction to Bell, who argues that growth in modern times comes from symbolic production (a game against persons) and no longer industrial production (a game of man against nature). Castells argues that knowledge and information processing were and are critical for both. What has changed is that corporations have simply increased the scope of their uses of information technologies. These changes produced a new world economy that is "informational, global, and networked" (Castells 2000:77). Capitalism and the information revolution coalesced into a network society where capitalism operates in real time.

As someone who could be considered a world systems theorist, Castells takes a more global view of capitalism and the Information Society.[4] For Castells, the economy of one country is interdependent on economic happenings across the globe. This is why he sees the economy of today as not qualitatively different than the economy of the past. Corporations that are most profitable are still those that make "things" and not "ideas". In other words, for every one Yahoo, there are ten Toyotas, and a country's wealth is still rooted in its industrial capacity. It is still, in Castells' eyes, a game of man against nature when we think globally. In this line of logic, it is possible to say that *for people in wealthy countries* such as Japan, France, and the United States it is a game of man versus man, but for the world it is still a game against nature. Furthermore, while people in wealthy countries are doing increasingly less manual labor, their wealth is still dependent upon the manual labor done in poorer countries, and the wealth extracted from those countries. In other words, a T-shirt in the US costs 10 dollars only because it is made for 50 cents in South Asia. And so, for Castells the Information Society does not mean there is a qualitative change in the world economy, only that the system of capitalism is more entrenched globally than it was fifty years ago, necessitating a global analysis of the system.

For this book, the major contribution of Castells is his concepts "space of flows" and "space of places". These two concepts necessarily follow from a world systems approach, as they emphasize the ability of spaces and groups to take advantage of networked ICTs and act globally, as opposed to other groups who are rooted in the physical environment and must act locally. The space of flows is defined as:

> "…the material organization of time-sharing social practices that work through flows. By flows I understand purposeful, repetitive, programmable sequences of exchange and interaction between physically disjointed positions held by social actors in the economic, political, and symbolic structures of society" (Castells 2000: 442).

So what does that mean exactly? I take "purposeful, repetitive, programmable sequences of exchange and interaction" as, simply, social patterns. I take "physically disjointed positions" to simply mean not in the same geographic location. And the "space" in which these flows can occur—indeed the only space they can occur—are through networked ICTs that compress space and time.

The space of flows can be characterized by three layers. The first layer is the material infrastructure, or the actual information and communication technologies themselves. These include broadcast towers, to servers, to fiber optic cables. This infrastructure removes "place" and replaces it with "process". The repeated patterns occur via ICTs, but there is no recognized space where these patterns occur. It is not a static location that matters. Instead, what matters here is the network of ICTs together and the flow of information through this network. This doesn't mean, then, that space is inconsequential. The second layer represents the space. Certain geographic locations, termed mega-cities by Castells, tend to either produce more information or perform important functions for the maintenance of the network. Examples of mega-cities are London, Tokyo, or New York. Other areas, not as dominant as these mega-cities, also play important roles in a given network, but are less important vis-à-vis the major centers. A hierarchy of importance emerges, where New York is a network hub, the sender and recipient of vast amounts of information, other places such as Washington, DC, and Chicago play important roles as nodes. Finally, the third layer is composed of people who are interacting in the spaces produced by ICTs. Individuals comprising this third layer are employed in the more important multinational corporations, government organizations, and academic institutions. In some ways, these individuals mirror the highly educated technocrats that Bell projected would become dominant in the political sphere. In Castells' formulation, these educated people are networked across nations, forming a "global elite" with different norms, values, and beliefs of those moored to their physical environment. These individuals "play a strategic role in shaping social practices and social consciousness for society at large" (2000: 442).

The space of flows is contrasted with the space of places, defined as "the historically rooted spatial organization of our common experience" (408–409). For most of human history, any given person would have consistently interacted in a circumscribed area. This area would have been infused with meaning, changing it from a homogenized space, to a unique *place*. The local corner store becomes the place where you met your first love; the local diner is where your seeing that person cheat on you began the move towards divorce, and so on. Further, this area is populated with people you know. The Millers down the street. The Jacksons up the hill. In this place people adopt unique norms that allow them to successfully navigate their place and provide meaning to their experiences. They become attached to this place, and value it.

Most people live their lives in this space of places:

> "The space of flows does not permeate down to the whole realm of human experience in the network society. Indeed, the overwhelming majority of people, in advanced and traditional societies alike, live in places, and so they perceive their space as place based" (453).

Castells' use of the phrase "permeate down" suggests a vertical relationhsip between these two spaces. The space of flows is dominant *over* the space of places. One space is tightly connected to the information flows vital to the capitalist enterprise, and is filled with cosmopolitan, educated, and technologically competent individuals. In a sense, this space is floating above its counterpart that is rooted in the parochial everyday experiences of life. The values and interests of the groups in these two spaces tend to run counter to each other, creating tension and ultimately conflict. Through this clash between those better positioned within the space of flows and those rooted in the spaces of places, Castells argues, we can understand a good deal of the cultural and political conflicts of the network society.

The second volume of the *Information Age* trilogy explores dimensions of these conflicts. For example, Castells analyzes the Mexican Zapatista social movement. The Zapatistas, rooted in the space of places, wish to retain their traditional farming and land-holding practices. The Mexican government, rooted in the space of flows, passed laws to position itself more favorably within the global trade network. These laws made their country more amenable to free trade but were disastrous for the Zapatistas. This same type of conflict—between people who are thinking ahistorical, global, and with an emphasis on capital accumulation and people who wish to retain their traditional patterns of life—reappear repeatedly according to Castells. The conflicts between the American government and vigilante enforcers of the Southwestern border, the Minutemen, are an example. The most notable example, however, would be the many Islamic movements against the encroachment of Western culture and values into their lands.

Like Daniel Bell, Manuel Castells practices a brand of techno-economic determinism, where economic changes, catalyzed by technological changes, are seen to produce changes in human values, beliefs. It was corporations, and their desire to maintain profit margins, that led to the wide-scale adoption of ICTs and the horizontal spread of corporations across the globe. This is not to say that Castells is not aware of the tremendous social and cultural changes underway in his network society. I outlined some of these changes above. However, these changes are seen as being consequences of economic changes.

Yochai Benkler's Nonmarket Production and Personal Freedom

Yochai Benkler (2006) argues in his seminal work *The Wealth of Networks* that we are living in a fundamentally different period of economic production. Many of the pronouncements of an Information Society in the 20th century, Benkler argues, were premature. Labeling our last century's economy as an "industrial information economy", he sees the 21st century, as the true beginning of a new age, one he labels a "networked information economy". This label is instructive, as it can be seen as an amalgamation of the emphases on information from Bell and networking from Castells. Differing from his predecessors, Benkler argues that the prime movers in this networked information economy are not corporations stretching across the globe looking for higher profit margins, but instead, the individual. Untethered from the necessity of corporations, people have more freedom to produce.

The logic underpinning the networked information economy can be summed up in two main ideas. First, in the networked information economy the primary type of economic production is human meaning and communication (this is similar to Bell, who argued that the new age is a game between persons, with the difference being that for Bell this game occurred within the confines of a corporate structure, while Benkler argues that the economies of scale afforded by corporations are no longer necessary). Second, the major physical capital needed to produce human meaning and communication is the personal computer and the Internet. The personal computer puts the means of production at one's fingertips, and the Internet is the low cost medium available to transmit what they have produced.

These characteristics make the networked information economy more diverse in the ways in which information is produced. With individuals being able to produce using personal computers, we have alongside more traditional market-oriented strategies to information production a number of nonmarket strategies. In particular collaboration and peer production allow for nonmarket products such as Wikipedia and the Linux operating system to proliferate. Because people are able to produce in more varied ways, the networked information economy provides more freedom for the individual person. Consider the education industry, of which I am a part. If, in the past, I wanted to find gainful employment as an educator, my only real option was to work in a brick and mortar institution. If I wanted to inspire young minds, the only way to do so was to navigate the bureaucratic hurdles of gaining the proper credentials, adopting the pose and presence of an educator and then putting myself on the market. There was just no realistic alternative. But, with today's technology, I can work with other knowledgeable people to produce a type of virtual school house. I and my cadre of knowledgeable people may not have the proper credentials, but we can still set up shop, hoping to make a difference through our knowledge of the material and our ability to captivate. The Khan Academy fits this mold. Or, even if I am with a school or university, I may decide that not enough or not enough categories of people have the privilege of experiencing a lesson from me. In this case, I can, under the auspices of my college provide a class were literally hundreds of thousands of people can take the class. The much talked about Massively Open Online Courses (MOOCs) fit this mold. These alternative ways of producing can be more effective than traditional, big-business led, market-oriented approaches. As evidence of this, Benkler cites Wikipedia and the Linux. The former being widely considered a superior option to almost any other encyclopedia, and the latter being adopted by many businesses over more well-known operating systems.

There are two ideas from the *The Wealth of Networks* that I will incorporate into future sections of this book. The first is the unique qualities of information. One unique quality of information is that it is a "nonrival" good, meaning, that it is an inexhaustible resource. If I read a magazine article or watch a television shown, it can still be enjoyed by someone else. Food and fuel, by contrast, are rival goods. Their consumption by one person means that the good is no longer usable by someone else. Nonrival goods, when made freely available after their production are considered public goods. Second, information is "both input and output of its own production process" (Benkler 2006:37). Doing academic research, writing songs, and producing computer software, requires access to previous works. For example, my ability to write this chapter is wholly contingent upon my access to what previous scholars, including Benkler, have done on this subject. Benkler argues that these two characteristics imply a reconsideration of strong copyright laws, as these laws are inefficient, and retard innovation. I will return to this in Chapter 8, where I argue for a growth in the nonmarket sector of the digital environment.

The second idea from Benkler is the argument surrounding personal freedom in the realms of culture and politics. With respect to culture, Benkler argues that individual freedom occurs via symbolic production online:

> "My claim is that the emergence of a substantial nonmarket alternative path for cultural conversation increases the degrees of freedom available to individuals and groups to engage in cultural production and exchange…" (2006: 293)

Institutions are losing their control over the type and tenor of cultural products. For example, he discusses how the music companies that flourished in the 20th century, with its monopoly on cultural production, displaced folk culture. The communication technologies of the 20th century were powerful, but required large amounts of capital investments to be harnessed. The means to produce and disseminate cultural products were reserved to those few people or groups that could own and operate television and radio stations or record companies. These businesses, oriented towards the market, produced and disseminated homogeneous cultural products to the masses in order to recoup their investment. In this way, commercial mass culture replaced folk culture in the 20th century. However, in the 21st century, nonmarket peer production is allowing a resurgence of folk culture, because the freedom to produce culture has been handed back to the masses.

The shift in power from large institutions to individuals also underlies the changes in the political realm. The direction of power is moving from states to people, Benkler argues. The Internet aids in democratization because news organizations must now contend with individuals and small groups producing their own news stories and interpretations of events. Also, states have a difficult time controlling information on the Internet because, as a purely technical matter, the Internet has far too many points of entry and too many connections. While the Internet does not lead directly to democratization, its architecture gives more people more chances to enter into the discourse on political issues.

In sum, Benkler's concept of the networked Information Society describes the change in modern, technologically advanced societies from a top-down, centralized mode of production to an economy that is based on distributed individual production of meaning. This change has occurred because of the technological advances of ICTs, leading to mass ownership of personal computers and mass subscriptions to Internet service. Now, individuals can produce economic goods, cultural products, and political opinion freed from the constraints of corporations and nation states.

First and foremost, *The Wealth of Networks* is about the transformation of the *market*.[5] As such its techno-economic determinism is inevitable—transformation in ICTs and the economy lead to changes in the cultural and political realms. Like Bell, Benkler attempts to avoid the assertion that his ideas are deterministic. He writes:

"Neither deterministic nor wholly malleable, technology sets some parameters of individual social action. It can make some actions, relationships, organizations, and institutions easier to pursue, and others harder. In a challenging environment…it can make some behaviors obsolete by increasing the efficiency of directly competitive strategies. However, within the realm of the feasible…different patterns of adoption and use can result in very different social relations that emerge around technology" (2006: 17–18).

In this way, Benkler avoids the naked, first-level techno-economic determinism. But Benkler is guilty of a more subtle type of determinism. For Benkler, freedom amounts to the *freedom to produce for the economy*. While his ideas on nonmarket production are brilliant, and I will apply his ideas to a great extent in later chapters, I am left feeling that too much of human phenomena are left unexamined. Can collaboration be used at an everyday level to, say, organize a picnic? Yes. Can disadvantaged groups use the personal freedom of information production to work outside of institutions in order to build identity? Yes, of course. It is these types of phenomena that are overlooked.

CONCLUSION

In this chapter I discussed three models of the Information Society. These models explain a lot about our current world. They go a long way towards explaining the tremendous economic and technological changes and what they mean for society. Bell identified the importance of information manipulated by computers as the defining element of our time. I see Bell's notion of the centrality of theoretical knowledge as the key takeaway. Castells understood that it was the ability of corporations to network and exchange this information without regard for space and time that produced power in today's age. The space of flows—spaces of places dichotomy is quite useful, as it provides a conceptual framework for understanding many of the conflicts in today's society. And Benkler, writing from the vantage point of Web 2.0 and near ubiquitous computing, understood that it is the ability of the everyday person to possess Bell's computers and be a part of Castells' networks that will produce freedom for the individual in today's society. Benkler's understandings of the growth in nonmarket production and the personal freedom associated with it will be a topic I return to frequently in the chapters ahead.

Despite the accomplishments of these theorists and what these models explain, I believe that these models deflect our attention away from important phenomena. This includes how inequality is produced and reproduced, how we are socialized into our class and racial identities, how institutions hinder and aid our progress, and the process of family formation from dating to marriage to divorce, among others. In order to fully grasp the profound social changes in our world today, we need to refocus our lens on these sociological phenomena. The perspective I will introduce in later chapters of this book will help with this refocusing. However, there is another lens that must also be addressed—the digital divide. That will be the focus on the next chapter.

CHAPTER TWO

The Digital Divide

INTRODUCTION

In the last chapter I discussed one lens through which we understand the 21st century—the popular Information Society models. In this chapter I discuss a second lens—the digital divide metaphor. In the strictest sense, the notions surrounding the digital divide are derived from Information Society models, and therefore repeat some of the same arguments. Mainly, the changes in everyday social interactions and culture are downplayed, and the focus is on the technological and the economic. The digital divide, being such an easily digestible metaphor, has become more ingrained into the thought processes of the media and policy makers than Information Society models. I will briefly discuss the history of the digital divide, moving from early public dialogue about access to Information and Communication Technologies (ICTs) to more current debates about users' skills at using ICTs. After discussing the history, I will outline three problems I have with this metaphor. I end the chapter by showing how views on ICTs are distorted because of the digital divide lens.

UNDERSTANDING THE DIGITAL DIVIDE

The First Digital Divide

In 1995, the National Telecommunications and Information Administration (NTIA) issued a report entitled, "Falling through the Net: A Survey of the 'Have Nots' in Rural and Urban America" (National Telecommunications and Information Administration 1995). The report concluded that American society vis-à-vis technology could be divided into two groups. One group owned ICTs, and was termed the "haves". The latter group, people in rural areas, minorities, and people with low incomes, were labeled the "have nots". The report used a metaphor describing this gap between the haves and have nots as a "Digital Divide". The metaphor had a seductive simplicity to it, and society's leaders latched onto it.

President Bill Clinton made addressing this digital divide a priority of the White House. In his 1996 State of the Union Address, Clinton pronounced that "In our schools, every classroom in America must be connected to the information superhighway, with computers and good software, and well-trained teachers" (National Archives and Records Administration, 1996). For Clinton and other leaders at the time, the digital divide meant that some people could not get onto the "information superhighway". This is a somewhat antiquated term, but at that time it held great symbolic weight as a metaphor in its own right. In the static era of Web 1.0[1], the Internet was then about access to information—government documents and educational resources, as opposed to now where the Internet is just as much about interaction with others and the manipulation of information.

The digital divide was on the minds and lips of people outside of the White House as well. An article in the *New York Times* entitled "A New Gulf in American Education, the Digital Divide" detailed the differences in life chances between two boys attending schools no more than one mile apart in Silicon Valley (Poole 1996). One student, nestled in a prestigious private school, had the latest technology at his fingertips. The other, languishing in an impoverished public school, had to share one computer with an entire student body of 500. The article goes on to say:

> "The digital divide between these two schools in the heart of Silicon Valley provides perhaps the most striking example anywhere in the nation of a widening gap—between children who are being prepared for lives and careers in the information age, and those who may find themselves held back".

Not only did the student in the wealthy school have access to more hardware, but the way in which he was allowed to use the computer was qualitatively better than the student in the poor district. The article quotes Stanford professor of education (now emeritus) Michael Kirst:

> "The way computers are used in the classroom—and the way the Internet will change their use—is really a profound commentary on education.... The Internet is a prophetic example: richer kids with access to a home computer and to the Internet can use it as a means of exploration and discovery. Poorer kids without the Internet will just use a computer, in the classroom, for drill-and-practice exercises" (Poole 1996).

That same year, the *New York Times* ran another article about a cash-strapped library in Georgia waiting on a decision from the federal government on funding subsidies for Internet access (Lohr 1996). Congress had already decided that schools and libraries should get discounts on their Internet subscriptions, and an eight-member board was set up to decide how much would be given (a still-running program that would eventually be called E-Rate). The article goes on to say that poor communities, like the one in Georgia, will need a discount in order to provide Internet service to people in the community. The article concludes by saying that this is a small step, and that "more than discount-rate telecommunications services, to be sure, will be needed to help close the digital divide between wealthy and poorer communities" (Lohr 1996).

In subsequent reports by the NTIA, the sentiment that American society was fast becoming divided by a gap in information technology solidified: "Groups that were already connected (e.g., higher-income, more educated, White and Asian/Pacific Islander households) are now far more connected, while those with lower rates have increased less quickly. As a result, the gap between the information 'haves' and 'have nots' is growing over time" (NTIA 1999). Harvard professor Henry Louis Gates (1999) weighed in on the digital divide from an African American standpoint, asserting that "Today we stand at the brink of becoming two societies, one largely white and plugged in and the other black and unplugged". And, "The Internet is the 21st century's talking drum, the very kind of grass-roots communication tool that has been such a powerful source of education and culture for our people since slavery".

While no substantial benefits had been measured for those who had access to information technology at that moment, society's leaders in the 1990s predicted that those benefits would be forthcoming. The "haves" could remain active in a society that was increasingly moving its political, economic, and educational activities online. Meanwhile, the "have nots" would be left behind, attempting to thumb a ride onto the information superhighway.

The Second Digital Divide: Digital Inequality

Just a decade and a half after the digital divide became a national concern, the technological landscape had changed. Scholars had begun to abandon research on simple access and moved towards a focus on how people use ICTs. The gap between those who had and those who had not was evaporating. There were two main reasons for this.

First, ICTs had gotten cheaper, and had decreased in cost relative to other comparable goods. In the 1980s through the mid 90s, a personal computer was a luxury, owned primarily by academics and families in the middle and upper class. However, the costs of personal computers have steadily declined since then. Today a lower-end personal computer is well within the reach of working class homes. At the same time, Internet access became less expensive and more ubiquitous. Once the federal government allowed private businesses access to the Internet in the mid-1990s[2], service providers scrambled to open up new markets. Through now irrelevant or defunct companies like America Online and Prodigy, Americans gained Internet access via telephone lines. A more profound change occurred with wireless Internet services and the grafting of Internet service onto the mobile phone. This made Internet access available to even more groups who have been seen as disadvantaged with respect to Internet access, especially African Americans and Hispanics (Smith 2010).

A second reason for the move away from studies of pure access was the rapid innovations in user-friendly software and hardware. This began in earnest in the 1980s. These innovations made it easier for people without computer backgrounds to extract benefits from ICTs. The mouse made it possible to point and click, the visual icons on a desktop made it easier to access programs, and web browsing software made it easier for users to find content on the Internet. Without these innovations in the 1980s and early 1990s, computing would have remained restricted to academics and a small set of people who could invest the necessary amount of time in learning code. These innovations have continued in the 21st century, and one of the primary selling points of touchscreen tablet computers, especially the iPad, have been their user friendliness.

Because of these changes—the decreased cost of computing and the growth of user-friendly hardware and software—the digital divide metaphor in its original conception lost much of its explanatory power in academic circles.[3] People across class, racial, and gender lines were enjoying access to computers, Internet, and mobile phones. Scholars began to understand that the most important differences between groups are with respect to knowledge and skill. City University of New York professor and early technology scholar Paul Attewell recognized this new area of difference as a "second digital divide" (Attewell 2001), and some scholars, including myself, have taken to using the term "digital inequality" (DiMaggio et al. 2004).

This second digital divide is, again, a metaphor, for the gap between the haves and have nots. Only this time the gaps are more numerous. The most parsimonious way to think of this second-level digital divide is as a divide in skills. But this begs the question of what are skills and which skills are relevant? The second digital divide can mean the gap between those who know how to add symbolic content to the digital environment (creating and uploading YouTube videos, writing a blog and manipulating tags and keywords to make that blog more visible in search engines) and those who don't. It can mean the gap between those who understand the concept of a digital footprint, and take steps to control the information they make available online and those who don't. It can mean the gap between people who know where to go online for legitimate information and those who don't. The main point here is that once access is achieved there are still those who "have" and those who "have not".

Table 2.1. Digital Divide Typologies

Mossberger et al. (2003)	Warschauer (2003)	Van Dijk (2005)
Access (owning technology)	Physical Resources (ownership)	Motivational Access (attitudes that lead to the usage of technology)
Skills (technical competence and literacy)	Digital Resources (relevant topics and language)	Material Access (possession of technology)
Opportunity (beliefs about computers and achievement)	Human Resources (education)	Skills Access (possession of digital skills)
Democratic (beliefs about how technology enhances civic engagement)	Social Resources (support systems and Internet communities)	Usage Access (possession of a diversity of applications, and the time to use these applications)

Because the notion of "skills" is too broad, scholars have introduced a myriad number of labels to identify each type of divide (Table 2.1). For example, Mark Warschauer (2003), using field work on rural Indians' uses of computers, argues that there is a divide in social support: some people are in environments that are conducive to the adoption of technologies and others simply are not. Similarly, Jan Van Dijk (2005), one of the more critical thinkers about the digital divide, argues that there are at least four dimensions upon which groups can be divided. Along with the aforementioned access and skill divides, groups can also be divided based upon their motivation and the diversity of uses of their ICTs. These scholars are on to something. But in my view, there attempts at better specifying uneven engagement in the digital environment are derailed by importing the "have" and "have not" metaphor. I believe it is the metaphor itself that is the problem and needs to be done away with entirely. I will turn to this argument in the next section.

THE PROBLEM(S) WITH THE DIGITAL DIVIDE METAPHOR

The digital divide metaphor has achieved hegemonic status. It is used by journalists, academics, politicians, and others to describe the uneven adoption and usage of ICTs. In some ways, the metaphor has been more than useful as its simplicity provides a beacon to which disparate interest groups can navigate towards. People understand "gap", "have", "have not", and "bridges" quite easily. Further, there are obvious and measurable differences between rich and poor, black and white, and so on, adding credence to the metaphor. When its abstract simplicity is combined with the concrete obviousness of differences seen on the ground, the metaphor takes on a flavor of "common sense". However the digital divide conceals as much as it reveals. In order to show this, I discuss three problems I see with the metaphor. I think each problem, in its own way, contributes to the obfuscation of the social and cultural phenomena associated with ICTs.

A Problem of Definition

One problem with the digital divide metaphor is that it is open to too many interpretations. Several scholars have also made this point (McSorely 2003, van Dijk 2005). When we say "digital" that can mean anything related to modern technology. Most devices in modern life fall into the category of digital: personal computers, Internet, mobile phones, software applications for computers and mobile phones, MP3 players, DVD players, and even your coffeepot and washing machine. This is a minor aspect of the problem. The most pressing concern is that when we say "divide" we are not entirely sure of the basis for which we have a divide. Clearly there can be many divides. Is it ownership (the first digital divide)? Is it quality of usage (the second-level digital divide)? Well, how do we measure quality? Is it, like the measurements used by the International Telecommunications Union, a statistical construct combining measures of access, usage, and skills of users?[4]

For scholars, operationalizing a concept is an occupational hazard. But the divide is just as much an academic concern as it is a public one, and the metaphor's elasticity allows it to be stretched to any number of situations to fit the whims of any number of entities. Scholars are aware of this, and are cautious about drawing conclusions. But others in society are not. Because the divide has no clear definition, it can be defined as any group pleases.

For example the 2009 Recovery and Reinvestment Act set aside $7.2 billion to bridge the divide in broadband access across the country. (This is discussed more in Chapter 7.) These divides are most acute in rural areas and in low income communities, and providing broadband to these groups is a laudable goal. On the Federal Communications Commission (FCC) website, the benefits of providing access to rural areas were estimated to include 500,000 new jobs, an increase in economic growth of $50 billion annually, and a 6–8% increase in graduation rates for those households who gain access to broadband (FCC 2012). While we may not be exactly sure to what degree not having broadband access retards the social mobility or hinders the amount of participation in civil society for rural residents (see the second problem discussed below), most scholars agree that access to broadband technology is critical to tapping into the benefits offered by the Information Society. This is an example of a divide in access, and it needs to be bridged.

But now consider this article published in *PC Magazine* entitled "Guiding Women across the Digital Divide" about a nonprofit program called Per Scholas located in the Bronx, New York (Lynn 2012). The article focuses on how the nonprofit teaches women computer coding and networking skills necessary for work in the computer industry:

> "It's no great revelation that there's a scarcity of women and minorities in the science, engineering, and technology sectors....Yet, the technology demographic continues to change (slowly but surely), becoming more diverse, particularly when it comes to the IT workforce.... I had the chance to speak at the graduation of 17 exceptional women from all walks of life who had the perseverance and fortitude to endure a rigorous 15 weeks of training that prepared them for A+, MCTS, MCITP, and networking certifications. Just about every graduate had already received her A+ cert by the time of graduation, one had already obtained her networking certification, and the rest were preparing to take the required tests."

The idea here is that there is a divide between men and women, especially low income women, in the information technology sector. Insofar as women have been prevented from pursuing careers in technology because of discrimination, nonprofits like the one detailed in this article can be a way for low income women to move into the technology industry. But it is a stretch to apply the label "digital divide" to this phenomenon and a stretch to consider training women for careers in the tech industry an instance of bridging the digital divide. There are certainly fewer women majoring in science and technology on college campuses, and fewer women working in the tech industry, but this is far removed from these women not having access to ICTs or not knowing how to use them. It may be better to consider a program like Per Scholas to be bridging a gender gap produced by the ideology that women are not as good as men in science and math. But this is how the lack of a clear definition allows the term to be stretched to any number of situations.

The problem of definition creates difficulties when developing solutions for addressing the digital divide, especially in the political arena. Without an agreed-upon public understanding of just what the digital divide is or what type of divide is most important, resources may be diverted to areas that, while well meaning, are simply not addressing any type of differences in ICT access or usage. Alternatively, real and significant divides—especially as they relate to nonmarket uses of ICTs—may go unnoticed because more easily identifiable, economic interests garner more attention. People can readily attach onto the lack of ownership, but may find it hard to imagine that there is a divide in symbolic content production. However the latter divide may prove to be of more significance than the former.

A Problem of Evidence

There are common themes in the digital divide literature. Research clearly showed a first-level, or access, divide between "haves" and "have nots". In the mid-1990s people with lower levels of educational attainment, lower incomes, and minorities had lower rates of ownership (Bucy 2000), and although by the year 2000 those differences were still significant, they had already begun to shrink (Katz et al., 2001). With these differences in access shrinking, scholars dutifully moved on to the second-level digital divide of usage. Research clearly shows divides here as well (DiMaggio et al. 2004). For example, research has shown that users with greater levels of education and hailing from more privileged backgrounds have more knowledge of web browsing (e.g., understanding of preference settings and file extensions like .jpg and .pdf) and are more likely to visit sites that increase political participation and job opportunities (Hargitaii and Hinnant 2008).

So there is clear evidence for the many, many divides. But there is a lack of evidence that links these cross-sectional, points-in-time measures with *future* consequences. Longitudinal studies that assess the effect of being a "have not", however it is defined, are few. Those available studies show little evidence that there is any consequence. A study done on Internet use and civic engagement

(Jennings and Zeitner 2003), while a bit dated having been done in the early 2000s, is instructive. The study found that there is a correlation between Internet use and interest in public affairs. However, when the researchers took into account the political and civic interests of respondents they found the effect of using the Internet was negligible. A second study is equally revealing. A longitudinal analysis of students from kindergarten to third grade also found the relationship between lack of computers and academic achievement minimal (Judge et al. 2006). In that study the subject pool was divided into those who attended high poverty schools and those who attended low poverty schools. Computer use and academic achievement of over 8000 students over several years were assessed. The study found some evidence of a first-level divide, showing that children in low poverty schools have more access to home computers than did children in high poverty schools. Schools had done a good job of equalizing the home difference within the school however, as by the time the children had reached third grade there were no differences in school access. The study also found some evidence of a second-level divide, as students in high poverty schools used the computer more for reading, while students in low poverty schools used computers to browse the Internet. *But were there any consequences for children because of these divides?* No. The study concluded that "more frequent computer use among low-achieving readers from both economic groups did not result in academic gains" (Judge et al. 2006: 58).

It is possible that I have overlooked some studies, or studies are nearing completion as I write these pages. But one should not have to look so hard or wait so long. It has been approximately 30 years since personal computers became available to large portions of American society. It has been 20 years since scholars began identifying differences in Internet access and the Clinton administration made Internet access one of their foci. The mass availability of mobile phones has been a reality for 10 years. Yet, we still have no clear understanding of the price people pay for their comparative lack of access or skill. We cannot say something to the effect of "using the Internet periodically increases one's income by...over a ten-year period", or "for each year a child goes without a home computer, his GPA decreases by 0.5 when compared to a child who has a home computer".

This doesn't mean that the consequences of not having Internet access or not having knowledge of how to operate ICTs are non-existent. Because there are few studies available proves only that there are few studies available. It may be that the cost in time and money of collecting longitudinal data is prohibitive for most scholars. It may also mean that the Internet usage, skills, class, race, and geography are impossibly intertwined. But most community leaders and scholars are not taking this critical stance.[5]

A Problem of Ideology

The third problem with the digital divide is ideological. The divide is racialized. The metaphor is wrapped in notions of white-advantage, minority-disadvantage, white technological progress and minority primitiveness. Minorities *must* be disadvantaged in the arena of technology in the same way that they are lagging behind in income, wealth, and educational attainment.

The Pew Research Center's Internet and American Life Project has compiled the most comprehensive collection of quantitative studies on digital trends in America. It is the first place I go to look for reliable information on information technology in the same way that a demographer would go to the Census. In 2010 the organization published research showing that minorities use the mobile phone more and for more diverse purposes than whites.[6] I quote a segment from this research at length:

> "The story I've been telling so far is one where minorities either trail (or are at parity with) whites, but the story is much different when we look at the use of mobile technologies—especially mobile phones. Both blacks and English-speaking Latinos are more likely to own a mobile phone than whites. Foreign-born Latinos trail their Native-born counterparts in cell phone ownership, but this gap is significantly smaller than the gap in internet use between these groups.
>
> Moreover, minority adults use a much wider range of their cell phones' capabilities. Compared with white cell phone owners, blacks and Latinos are significantly more likely to use their mobile devices to:
>
> - Text message (70% of all African Americans and English-speaking Latinos use text messaging, vs. just over half of whites)
> - Use social networking sites
> - Use the Internet
> - Record and watch videos
> - Make a charitable donation via text message (this finding is particularly interesting since white Internet users are more likely to have made a charitable donation online—25% of online whites have done so, compared with 17% of African Americans and 14% of Latinos.)
> - Use e-mail
> - Play games
> - Listen to music
> - Use instant messaging
> - Post multimedia content online

The reason why I post such a long quote is to show in detail the ways in which traditionally disadvantaged minorities are outpacing whites in their usage of mobile technology. This is not simply a matter of ownership or frequency of use. Minorities are far more aggressive in their use of mobile phones and in extracting benefits from their mobile phones. This was not a quirk. Figure 2.1 shows data from a second survey done in 2012. Respondents were asked if they own a cell phone, and if they did any of a series of activities with their cell phone. For all activities from the most mundane to higher end activities, minorities are outpacing whites.

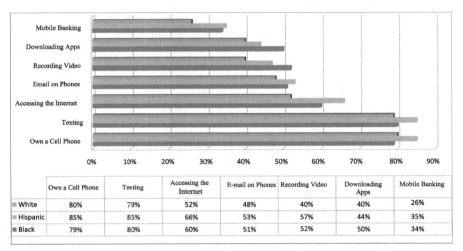

	Own a Cell Phone	Texting	Accessing the Internet	E-mail on Phones	Recording Video	Downloading Apps	Mobile Banking
White	80%	79%	52%	48%	40%	40%	26%
Hispanic	85%	85%	66%	53%	57%	44%	35%
Black	79%	80%	60%	51%	52%	50%	34%

Figure 2.1. Cell Phone Activities for Racial Groups in 2012*.

*From: "Cell Phone Activities 2012", Pew Internet and American Life Foundation—http://pewinternet. org/~/media//Files/Reports/2012/PIP_CellActivities_11.25.pdf, Accessed May 19, 2013).

These findings have not been seen as a digital divide with minorities being the "haves" and whites being the "have nots". On the contrary, this disparity in mobile phone usage is interpreted as a potential *disadvantage* for minorities! Pew published a report one year later entitled "For minorities, new 'digital divide' seen".[7] Again, I quote at length:

> "Today, as mobile technology puts computers in our pockets, Latinos and blacks are more likely than the general population to access the Web by cellular phones, and they use their phones more often to do more things.
>
> But now some see a new "digital divide" emerging—with Latinos and blacks being challenged by more, not less, access to technology. It's tough to fill out a job application on a cellphone, for example. Researchers have noticed signs of segregation online

that perpetuate divisions in the physical world. And blacks and Latinos may be using their increased Web access more for entertainment than empowerment…

[M]obile Internet access may not be the great equalizer. Aaron Smith, a Pew senior research specialist, says there are obvious limitations on what you can do on a mobile device—updating a resume being the classic example.

'Research has shown that people with an actual connection at home, the ability to go online on a computer at home, are more engaged in a lot of different things that people who rely on access from work, a friend's house, or a phone,' Smith says."

Apparently, this new divide is based on the inability of the mobile phone to accomplish the same tasks as a laptop. Here we see how the concept of "digital divide" is racialized. The notion that blacks and Hispanics may be outpacing whites is downplayed. It is given recognition, but there is no sense that whites are, in this instance, the "have nots". And to rub salt in the wound, the very advantage that minorities have is interpreted as a disadvantage, never mind the fact that most commentators on technology would say that the Internet experience will be dominated by mobile phones. This is the essence of the ideological problem seen in the raw.

In my view the ideological problem is the most damaging of the three. It masks the ways in which traditionally disadvantaged groups have been using ICT's aggressively to achieve their goals in life. The ways in which minorities have been using technology to their advantage is in many ways grounded in everyday cultural practices, but it is hard to "see" this given the digital divide lens. Instead, the digital divide repackages the narrative of a disadvantaged minority unable to succeed in modern society in a digitized 21st century wrapper. This ideology trickles into academia, bending research into finding more and more ways that minorities have fallen behind, while the ways in which they are aggressive participants in the digital environment are ignored.

THE DISTORTIONS OF THE DIVIDE

If the popular Information Society models I discussed in Chapter 1 *deflect* our attention away from social and cultural phenomena, then the digital divide lens *distorts* these phenomena, blurring them such that our focus is only ever on market-related divides. We start with a phenomenon that fits within the narrative produced by the Information Society. This phenomenon will inevitably be one that is tied to the economy (or technological skill as it relates to economic participation). Non-economic phenomena are usually overlooked, especially when they relate to the quotidian, everyday uses of ICTs. Next we make a comparison, usually of racial groups (with whites set as the standard by which other groups are compared), and social classes (with middle class users set as the standard). We will find a significant difference, and consider this as another example of a digital divide.

An appropriate study in this scheme, for example, would begin by measuring the ability of young people to write computer code. There is no agreed-upon measure of the digital divide (Problem 1), and so measuring differences in coding skill would be seen as an acceptable illustration. The importance of code-writing ability is given more credibility because it falls within the techno-economic frame produced by the Information Society models. We can readily see how being able to write computer code can translate into opportunities in the labor market. Next, the study would look at differences along class and racial lines, comparing middle class and whites to working class and minorities. My guess is that a study of this nature would find significant differences between social classes and racial groups, with middle class respondents and white respondents being more likely to have some knowledge of coding. The study could then be added to the wealth of "support" for a digital divide, even if the study is cross-sectional, and the differences in knowing code may not make a real difference in earnings at a future date (Problem 2). Furthermore, this would support our notions of minority inferiority (Problem 3).

The ability to write and manipulate computer code is a valuable skill, the possessing of which will increase one's value on the labor market. Furthermore, it is through computer code that we experience ICTs. The websites, software, and mobile applications we enjoy are all because people have written computer code. Later, in Chapter 7 I will talk about the importance of nurturing code writing for nonmarket purposes. However, studies employing the above scheme collectively produce an incomplete picture of our Information Society.

Writing computer code is not unlike being able to perform maintenance on an automobile during the Industrial Age. I can imagine that a person with this skill would have a great degree of leverage in the labor market, and her ability conferred a degree of status and a feeling of competence. All good things, and a racial and class divide in maintenance ability would mean a subsequent divide in those benefits. But the automobile is associated with many social and cultural transformations in American society, from a change in dating patterns to the suburbanization of society. Measuring ownership of cars (read: first-level digital divide) or skill in using or repairing one's car (read: second-level digital divide) gets us only marginally closer to understanding those social and cultural transformations. And so it is with ICTs in the Information Society. Studying digital divides does not get us closer to understand the countless ways people are using ICTs to accomplish goals in their everyday lives.

CONCLUSION

I began with a discussion of the digital divide as it relates to access, what has been called the first-level divide. This divide, at least in Western societies, is not as prominent as it once was, although politicians and laymen still think of the technological landscape in this way. Scholars see the next divide as one in digital skills, what can be called the second-level digital divide. Although the move from the first level to the second level brings with it a more accurate representation of reality, I still see problems with the metaphor. I outlined three of these problems above: the problems of definition, evidence, and ideology. The metaphor refers to everything and nothing at the same time, and there is no solid evidence tying disadvantage directly to the lack of ICTs. But most problematic, in my view, is that the metaphor is racialized and grounded in notions of minority disadvantage. These all lead to a distorted view of the Information Society, one where we are so busy pointing out divides related to the market that we ignore the nonmarket uses of ICTs by groups in society.

CHAPTER THREE

The Digital Practice Perspective

INTRODUCTION

In this chapter I explain the two main concepts that make up the digital practice perspective: "digital environment" and "digital practices". The digital environment is defined as the social space produced through interconnected information and communication technologies (ICTs). The digital environment, or DE, is distinct from the physical environment, or PE. It is a space where one must enter into via ICTs. Upon entry, one is faced with a new set of social forces, the navigation of which requires adopting new behaviors. Digital practices, then, are the behaviors that result when groups navigate the digital environment. It is ultimately the uncovering of these digital practices and exploring their consequences for the social structure of society that identifies a "digital practice perspective". This perspective, focusing on the everyday actions of groups in the digital environment, is meant to be a corrective to techno-economic determinism exhibited in the Information Society models and digital divide metaphors discussed in Chapters 1 and 2, respectively.

THE DIGITAL ENVIRONMENT

The notion of a digital environment is not new. Yochai Benkler (2006), whose writings inform a great deal of this work, uses the digital environment in his book

The Wealth of Networks. In Benkler's work it is used to describe the totality of technologies that interlink to produce the networked information economy. There is a colloquial use of the term as well. Writers and commentators may evoke the term digital environment when describing things that people do online (most often what they do on social networking sites like Facebook and Twitter).

My use of the term, in comparison to Benkler, denotes a different collection of phenomena. I am interested in the social interactions allowable by these technologies, and not the technology itself. In comparison to technology writers, my use of the term is more expansive. It is not only what is done online that matters—even though that is the most significant aspect. My use of the digital environment signifies the *social space* that individuals enter into when using ICTs. It is a space that emerges through a convergence of hardware, the software code used to animate this hardware, and the human norms that have developed around this hardware and software. The digital environment (DE), has a series of attributes that make it distinct from the physical environment (PE), and when individuals enter into this environment these attributes must be negotiated. In the paragraphs that follow I develop this notion further.

The DE as a Social Space

Allison Cavanagh (2007), in her review of Internet research, *Sociology in the Age of the Internet,* describes three general approaches to the study of the Internet. One approach is to consider the Internet primarily as a medium for communication. This approach is often taken by scholars in media studies, communication, or possibly political science. Studies may explore the production, dissemination, and consumption of information and the primary entities involved in the process. Second, a study can approach the Internet as a technology. In this approach, often taken by scholars in computer information systems or information technology, relevant questions revolve around the functions and properties of the Internet. A third approach, most often taken by scholars in psychology and sociology view the Internet as an environment for social interaction. Scholars who take this approach ask questions about the development of community and the construction of identity.

All three emphases are important, and studies might surely incorporate all three. But I will focus on the third emphasis, the Internet primarily as a social space. I take the standpoint that it is important to understand how the Internet as a technology produces this space, but the technology itself is secondary. Likewise, understanding how meaning is transmitted via text, images, and audio is an important part of understanding social relationships, but this is at best a component of a broader focus on what the transmission of meaning means for sociological processes.

Cavanagh was referring to the Internet, and specifically online phenomenon. But I want to extend this idea to all ICTs. The Internet, along with mobile phones, computers, tablet computers, social networking sites, and the like all work to produce one interconnected social space. This idea mirrors that of Castells' concept of the space of flows (see Chapter 1). We are accustomed to thinking of each device as producing its own mutually exclusive phenomena. And certainly each individual piece of hardware and block of software has its own set of properties. But these devices work together in most instances.

Consider how people converge through ICTs. Someone accesses the Internet wirelessly through their mobile phone in Nairobi, Kenya, making a comment on a social networking site like Google+, which is then seen by someone accessing the Internet through a landline connection in their office in Manchester, United Kingdom, who then replies to the comment, which is then seen by someone using a Wi-Fi connection on their tablet computer in the park in Kobe, Japan, who then links to the conversation on her personal blog, a blog whose contents are housed on servers in Copenhagen, Denmark.

Also, consider the degree of convergence between technologies. A company creates a website, and then repackages the website for a mobile phone application. Or, a movie is streamed to a computer via Netflix. Now because televisions and DVD players are equipped with computer processors and software applications, that same content is seen on these devices as well. Or think of someone writing an essay, using a word processing program. That person may write the essay offline, but then decide to upload that program to a company's server (in the cloud). Then someone in another city, using a different word processing program on a different computer using different hardware, downloads that essay and edits it.

Because of the convergence of people and technologies, we can think of all ICTs as producing a single space for social interaction. Thinking in these terms focuses the analysis squarely on the environment that is created. It is too easy, in this era of rapid technological advancement, to be mystified by technology and assume that each innovation produces a wholly new set of conditions. But in most cases, innovation does not produce entirely new phenomena. Mobile phones have gotten more powerful, the web has become more interactive, computers and the Internet have invaded all manner of appliances including watches and eyeglasses, but the social dynamics associated with these changes are quite the same as they were a decade ago. This is because these technologies produce a series of properties that change much more slowly than the technologies themselves. These properties will be discussed later in this chapter.

The Porous, Yet Discrete Space of the Digital Environment

There are similarities and differences between the DE and other types of environments that social scientists study such as the "urban", "rural", or "corporate" environment. Like these other environments, the boundaries of the digital environment are porous. People can move back and forth between a rural and urban environment, and they can do the same with the digital environment and the physical environment. Another similarity between the DE and other environments is the *reality* of it. Early conceptualizations of the Internet and cyberspace often framed computer-mediated interaction as being "virtual" and in some way inauthentic. This understanding seemed to crop up when conversations revolved around affective human interaction (as opposed to more practical information exchange). We tended to see phenomena such as online dating and the presentation of self to others as illusory.

But this understanding of the digital environment is inconsistent with our understandings of other types of environments. No one would suggest that people who move to the big city are somehow living a virtual existence, not as authentic as the rural environment. We just understand that the experience of living in a big city is "different". Or, a person who entered into a prison environment would certainly be in a very unusual social context, but his experiences are certainly not inauthentic. Most scholars would now suggest that the term virtual reality does a disservice to what happens in the digital environment, and I fall into that category. The digital environment is as real as any other environment in which people interact in.

Curiously, the analogy between the DE and other environments does not hold when it comes to the *degree* to which someone is a part of the environment. For example, one can characterize a business setting as being more or less indicative of a corporate environment, and thus that person is exposed to a greater or lesser degree to the effects of the corporate environment. This is even more obvious with urban environments, as some cities with higher population densities, greater diversity, and so on may expose their residents to more urban effects, than a person in a smaller city. But with the digital environment, you are either in it, or not. You are either using an ICT to interact with others, or not. In other words, the digital environment is porous, but discrete.

A question may arise: *What about when someone is given a lecture using Power-Point? Is this in the digital environment?* My answer would be, "depends". At most moments, there is no interaction occurring through the digitized media. The presenter is talking, and the attention is placed squarely on the presenter and when a reference is made to the screen, attention moves quickly to whatever media is showing, but there is no interaction occurring between presenter and audience or amongst audience members through the media. Now, consider a situation in which a presenter is giving instruction using a document in the cloud that is modifiable by others, such as Google Docs. Then, imagine that the presenter instructs the audience members to make changes together to the document. At that moment, the audience is in the DE. However, the presenter, unless she is following changes or modifying the document herself, is in the physical environment (PE).

And so what constitutes being in or out of the DE boils down to what our minds are focusing on. I like many professors must deal with students using laptops in my class. The students are, in their minds, multi-tasking—checking Facebook while at the same time listening to my lecture. I have a different interpretation of their actions. When students have focused their attention on me or others in the class, they are a part of the social space that is the physical environment. But the millisecond that they refocus their attention on communicating via smartphone or laptop they have left the physical environment and entered the digital environment. They cannot be in both spaces at the same time.

The Digital Environment Is Layered

Although we can consider ICTs to be interconnected and each to contribute to a single environment in which people interact, this does not mean, then, that all ICTs contribute equally to the explanation of any given social phenomenon. In order to integrate these two divergent assumptions—that ICTs create one social space and yet can have varying degrees of influence depending upon the phenomenon, we must take the approach that the DE is layered (Nuecthterlein and Weiser 2005, Zittrain 2008). Table 3.1 presents a model of how a layered digital environment can be envisioned, adapted from work by Jonathan Zittrain (2008). This is not the only possible model. As Zittrain also pointed out, other models can be constructed that are more or less nuanced. I have modified Zittrain's original model to fit the purposes of this present work. Seven layers are presented, starting at the level of infrastructure and ending with people.

The purpose of this layered model is to clue scholars in to the more salient influences on their phenomena of study. Different layers suggest different variables of study and the method most likely to produce an answer to their research question. Consider cyber bullying. The most salient layers, upon a cursory inspection, are the human layer (the interaction between people), the web layer (a web application like Facebook is needed to facilitate the interaction) and the content layer (some kind of image, text, or audio). Incorporating lower layers into one's analysis may only marginally increase the explanation. Alternatively, one may find that it is absolutely necessary to take the preceding layers into account. Consider a study comparing the amount of symbolic content uploaded to the Internet by nation. One may start, most obviously, with the content layer, and measure in some way the quantity of content present in the digital environment by nation. This is a good place to begin. However, exploring just the content does not get at the reasons for the disparity. It may be that nations populated by speakers who are not conversant in English, Spanish, French, or Chinese may find that software (software layer) and web applications (web layer) are not written for them, thus hindering their interaction in the digital environment. Also, a lack of hardware (hardware layer) and infrastructure (infrastructure layer) may be a prime cause for the unequal production of symbolic content.

Table 3.1. The Layers of the Digital Environment

Type of Layer	Description	Examples
Human	The direct communication between users	Building of social ties, cyber bullying, virtual community development
Content	The information that is produced and housed on the Internet	Documents, videos, music
Web	The programs that allow users to more easily use the Internet	Graphical User Interfaces (GUIs), Facebook, Google calendar, Farmville, mobile phone apps
Software	The programs that allow users to easily take advantage of computing powers of hardware	MS Excel, Internet Explorer, Firefox, Skype
Hardware	The types of machines that transmit and receive data	Computers, Mobile Phones, DVD players
Infrastructure	The wires or airwaves over which data is transmitted	Fiber Optic Cables, Wi-Fi Connections

THE PROPERTIES OF THE DIGITAL ENVIRONMENT

One of the major projects of French sociologist Emile Durkheim was the separation of sociology from psychology. Towards this goal, Durkheim ([1896]1982) wrote in *The Rules of the Sociological Method* about the type of phenomena that sociologists should concern themselves with. Durkheim called these phenomena "social facts". Durkheim describes social facts in this way:

"Here, then, is a category of facts which present very special properties: they consist of manners of acting, thinking and feeling external to the individual, which are invested with a coercive power by virtue of which they exercise control over him. Consequently, since they consist of representations and actions, they cannot be confused with organic phenomena, nor with psychical phenomena, which have no existence save in and through the individual consciousness. Thus they constitute a new species and to them must be exclusively assigned the term *social*" (p. 52).

This passage, undoubtedly one of the most discussed in graduate level sociological theory classes, is a good entry point for the ideas presented in this section. First, Durkheim describes the properties of the phenomena under question: manners of acting, thinking, and feeling that are external to the individual. Second, Durkheim argues that these phenomena have a causal effect (coercive power) over individuals. He argues that these social facts are different than the phenomena which are studied by biology or psychology, two disciplines which intuitively would seem to take into account these phenomena.

In this section I will talk about the collection of "facts" that define the digital environment. I'll use the more identifiable term *properties* going forward. These properties conform to the criteria set forth by Durkheim. First, they are unique to the digital environment and cannot be reduced to or found in other environments. Second, they have a coercive power to which individuals must adapt. These properties influence the social interactions that take place in the digital environment. These properties need to be understood when exploring social interaction in the digital environment. The properties I outline are not meant to be an exhaustive list. However, available research suggests that these properties are the most relevant to social processes online.

Property #1—The Decreased Cost of Manipulating Information

In the DE, the cost of manipulating information is far less than in the physical environment, to the point in some cases of being negligible. This notion is drawn from an understanding applied across disciplines that the Internet reduces transaction costs.[1] By manipulating information I mean producing, reproducing, and transmitting audio, text, and video. When we make a short video of our cat walking on two paws and upload it to YouTube, we have manipulated information. When we write an essay, this too is manipulating information. It simply costs us less to do these things in the Information Society. By cost, I mean everything needed to produce, reproduce, and transmit information, from the paper and ink to produce a book, to the technology one needs to purchase and the legal hoops one must jump through in order to start a radio station, to one's own physical labor or the money one expends for another person's labor. Daniel Bell, Manuel Castells, and Yochai Benkler all point to the importance of information in our current society. Primarily looking at it from an economic angle, they all argue that the ease of manipulating information has been the prime mover in changes in occupational structure, corporate expansion, and individual's ability to produce symbolic goods for the market.

But the greatest application of this property is at the everyday level of social interaction. Clay Shirky's *Here Comes Everybody: The Power of Organizing without Organizations* shows how this property can affect individuals in their everyday lives. Shirky argues that because the costs of manipulating information have been drastically reduced, people can form more groups for more purposes than ever before. Because the cost of manipulating information is lowered, people can do things with information simply because they want to. An example he gives is how a photo album of the annual Mermaid Day Parade in Coney Island is produced through individuals working together. It is quite easy to take a picture these days and upload it to a photo-sharing site like Flicker. It is also easy for computer programmers to write code that allows these photos to be catalogued through hash tags. By individuals doing something they already enjoy and would do anyway, people have a yearly photo album of the Mermaid Day Parade. In this way lowered cost of manipulating information has led to the formation of a greater number of groups.

Not only is the sheer number of groups increasing, but also there is a greater variety of groups forming. Again, this is because the DE lowers the cost of manipulating information. The majority of these groups are forming in the nonmarket sphere of activity. Taking photos of people dressed in weird costumes at a parade may be funny and interesting, but this activity in itself will most likely not produce a profit—few people would buy a magazine with these images. For this reason, no business has ever stepped in to compile these images.[2] However, in the DE, the costs of doing things are so low that people can afford to participate in group activities for intrinsic, non-economic reasons.

I imagine that the vast majority of people have contributed to a group activity without being aware of it (the costs of doing so are so low, we don't imagine we are contributing to anything substantial). Recently, I was at a conference held at my college. This was a relatively small conference, taking up only one large room. During the conference it was announced that if we wanted to make comments we should do so via Twitter using a certain hash tag. As the conference progressed people began to make comments and ask questions, eliciting responses from others. Often, pictures of presentation slides were taken and posted. Sometimes, when a presenter made a point that piqued someone's attention in the audience, they tweeted a link to a relevant website. My own contribution to the enterprise was to use a software program that extracted all the tweets associated with that hashtag and uploading them on a publicly available spreadsheet for later use. And there we were, doing all of this in the DE, simply because we could do it and we wanted to do it.

Each of us had to use our time and energy—albeit in tiny amounts—to collectively produce what was a neat compilation of the conference's most salient moments.

Shirky presents a typology of group activities, all of which are easier in the DE. I present a modified version of that typology in Table 3.2. The group activities run from the least difficult to accomplish (bottom row) to most difficult (top row). Sharing is the least difficult activity, and is illustrated by the example of the aforementioned Mermaid Day Parade. As we go up the scale, more is required from the participants. But still, the decreased cost of manipulating information makes these groups more likely to occur. Thus, with cooperating—let's say to produce a viable discussion of a small conference at a college—the user needs to be more committed to the activity, investing time in reading posts and responding to others. But still, these groups form easier. With collaboration, the synchronization of behavior is of a higher degree, with a site like Wikipedia setting up several rules for the editing of articles. Finally, collective action—what can be called the holy grail of group activity for sociologists—requires great commitment from those involved, in a sense putting their personal welfare in jeopardy for the sake of the group.

Table 3.2. Typology of Group Sharing Activities

Group Activity	Description	Examples
Collective Action	The final product requires a group effort, and the decisions made by the group are binding and have consequences for its members; the user's identity is tied to the group.	Protests initiated through ICTs, Flash robs
Collaboration	The final product requires a group effort and needs the synchronized production of many; collective decisions have to be made.	Open source software (Linux), Wikipedia
Cooperating	Synchronizing behavior in a mutual production of symbolic content.	Conversations on websites, IM, Twitter
Sharing	Producing content and sharing it on a public platform; a loose aggregate of individual productions.	Flickr

Property #2—The Digital Environment Allows Community without Propinquity

The digital environment allows people to interact and form bonds of sentiment without the constraints of space and time. This allows people within the digital environment to have "community without propinquity" (Calhoun 1998).[3] People committed to a social movement can commiserate across great distances. Or, on a less grand scale, mothers can now communicate with their children via text while she is at work and her progeny are at school.

This property works in conjunction with property number 1—as it is the manipulation of information that makes it possible to form a community. But communities are bonds of sentiment based on identity or group affiliation, and are not necessarily task based. The bonds created are also more durable. When we are a part of a community, there is a sense of "we" that lasts above and beyond any one meeting or task. In the college conference example I gave above, I may have felt a sense of "we" during the conference, but that feeling has long sense dissipated. I have no feeling that I belong to a group of "conference goers". Contrast this with a feeling one gets of being in a family, a racial group, a tight-knit neighborhood, and so on.

The ability to produce forms of community without propinquity is one of the more widely discussed properties of the digital environment. Beginning with Howard Rheingold's (1993) work *The Virtual Community: Homesteading on the Electronic Frontier*, academics and society at large have been fascinated by people's ability to communicate with a person with whom they do not share propinquity. Another instance of this property in practice is the literature on online diasporas. Diasporas are groups who have migrated from their country of origin and living as minorities in host countries. One can speak of the Lebanese diaspora or the Nigerian diaspora. Members of a diaspora are different from other migrant groups who assimilate into a host country and become indistinguishable from the majority group. Diaspora communities have a collective memory of their country of origin. They actively maintain ties with their homeland and discuss returning to that homeland.

One of the more thorough examinations of diaspora communities is the work done by Jennifer M. Brinkerhoff (2009), *Digital Diasporas: Identity and Transnational Engagement*. Brinkerhoff, in her analysis of several diaspora communities in the United States, shows how the Internet has assisted these communities as they navigate life in their host country. Members of these communities in the DE exchange practical knowledge needed to survive in the US, share personal successes and failures, and make connections with members of the community who did not immigrate. These are not communities in name only. Nor is it simply people who happen to be chatting to one another. In her analysis of two community websites in particular—one for Afghani immigrants called AfghanistanOnline and one for Somali immigrants called Somalinet, Brinkerhoff shows that diaspora communities in the DE exhibit the same characteristics as communities in the PE (Brinkerhoff 2009: 85–115). Rules for behavior, though minimal, are instituted and enforced. Bonds between members are created and nurtured. The identity of members are checked by others and verified. There is a sense of "we" that develops.

Despite the work of scholars like Brinkerhoff, online communities are often deemed a poor substitute for offline communities. Some simply do not see the interaction that occurs via ICTs as being of the same quality as interaction occurring when physical space is shared. Sherry Turkle (2011), in her book *Alone Together*, argues that even though ICTs connect us more than ever, these connections are hollow. The types of intimacy found through ICTs are, for Turkle, a type of fool's gold. She argues that we have the impression that connecting through e-mail, social networking sites, and mobile phones brings us closer together. However, she continues, the reliance on connections through these means drives us further apart. These connections, for Turkle, are not as fulfilling as "real" connections in the physical environment. We are alone even as we forge togetherness through ICTs.

But those who agree with Turkle are in the minority. Most scholars take the view that communities in the digital environment are not "virtual" in the sense that they are unreal or have a lesser impact on people than offline communities. Instead, scholars explore the *degree* to which a website and its collection of users can be understood as a community. A useful rubric has been provided by Nancy Baym (2010: 72–98), and is summarized in Table 3.3. If one believes that the qualities listed in Table 3.3 are sufficient for community development (these qualities listed by Baym are quite standard and uncontroversial), then a following question would be to what extent a given collection of people in the DE exhibit these qualities. This is indeed a valid question, but very different than saying that anything done in the DE is inauthentic or lesser than simply because it is done there.

Table 3.3. Qualities of Communities

Quality	Description
Sense of Space	People who are involved in communities think of it as a space
Shared Practice	People in online communities share "cultures" (norms, values, beliefs, symbols)
Shared Resources	People in online communities share resources in their communities (information, esteem, emotional, and a feeling that they are needed)
Shared Identities	A shared sense of who "we" are, such that regulars take on specific roles and share a social identity (race, profession, etc.)

I take time to address the realness of virtual communities because I have a sense that both scholars and the society at large see anything done online as fun and games, and somewhat less worthy of study. I place the blame squarely on the deflections produced by the Information Society lens and the distortions of the digital divide lens. Both perspectives make it difficult to see the validity of non-economic, everyday behavior. But the DE is much more than "liking" on Facebook and watching Youtube videos.

Property #3—Social Networks Are Ahistorical and Multidimensional

The term social network has become very popular, almost faddish, in the new millennium. In 2003, the *New York Times* called social network one of the new ideas of 2003 (Gertner 2003). The rise of social media platforms such as Facebook and Twitter are at the heart of this surge in the interest of social networks. One could easily come to the conclusion that "networking" is a term unique to the Information Society. However, Charles Kadushin (2011) writes that networks are not a new idea, and that humans have been embedded in relationships—the type of reciprocal relationships—we call social networks throughout history. He writes that social networks:

> "[H]ave been at the core of human history since we were hunters and gatherers. People were tied together through their relations with one another and their dependence on one another. Tribes, totems, and hierarchies may have come later. Kinship and family relations are social networks. Neighborhoods, villages, and cities are crisscrossed with networks of obligations and relationships" (2011:3).

Social networks are certainly not new. But within the DE, the qualities of social networks have changed. *They are more complicated.*

First, DE networks are ahistorical to a greater extent than networks in the PE. By ahistorical, I mean that the removal of face-to-face communication produces a relative indifference to physical status markers and the historical expectations associated with these statuses. The ascribed statuses that sociologists understand as ordering everyday interaction—class, race, gender, and increasingly sexual orientation—matter less for the building of networks in the DE. People across these lines can connect. The Hispanic male from the Bronx with an interest in anime can interact with the Asian female from San Jose. These two may not become friends *per se*, but they can navigate and interact in the same space. These temporary connections are called weak ties in the sociological literature, and I will discuss the importance of these ties in Chapter 5.

Ahistoricity does not mean that these statuses do not matter, only that they have less of an impact in the DE than in the physical environment. This also does not mean that networks are random, or based totally on access. In the lingo of social network analysis, networks are created based on similarity, or homophily (McPherson et al. 2001). However, the similarities are based less on older divisions of class, race, and gender—and more on new divisions of lifestyle (like the anime example above) and social issues (supporters of gay marriage, white supremacists).

Another attribute of networks in the DE is that they are more multidimensional than networks based in the physical environment. There are more connections between entities, and these connections come from a variety of places. The high school student can have a connection with his peers, but also his teachers, students from other schools, as well as people of different genders, races, and classes. There are few instances where a person who is in the DE cannot connect with someone else in the DE. In the language of social network analysis, networks in the DE have potentially less structural holes (Burt 1995).

To make this clear, let's consider a network in the physical environment. Think of a high school organized into various cliques. Now imagine there are two cliques—jocks and geeks. In the physical environment, there may be no direct connection between the members of each clique. They shun each other, or simply do not socialize in similar environments. If they are connected, it may be through a few individuals—those rare athletic geeks (or geeky athletes) who can associate with both cliques. And so any knowledge generated in one clique may never migrate to the other. This is called a structural hole—were it not for those supremely talented teenagers who excel at both AP Calculus and can dunk a basketball—those two cliques would have no connection.

Now consider any given individual in the DE. Simply by entering the DE, a user can potentially have a direct connection to every other user. There are few structural holes—at least in theory. Information can flow through millions of channels. Information is hard to control. This is the seminal problem for authoritarian regimes who want to control the type of information their citizens consume. The "great firewall of China", is nothing more than a structural hole, where the Chinese government acts as broker between international content and Chinese citizens (Goldsmith and Wu 2006, Mackinnon 2012).

Property #4—The Digital Environment Enables and Constrains through Code

The uses of technology are not set in stone. Nor, however, are they completely malleable. Technology is enabling and constraining, and different behaviors can sprout around the same technology. I use this basic premise and place it within the context of a digital environment, where code—the instructions given to hardware and software—is used to enable and constrain social interaction.

Lawrence Lessig (2011) famously wrote that "code is law". The expression is now bordering on the iconic. Unlike in the PE where man must understand laws and processes not of his making (e.g., the laws of motion or evolution), the digital environment is produced by humans and so are the laws of interaction. Computer programmers determine what a user can and cannot do:

> "We can build, or architect, or code cyberspace to protect values that we believe are fundamental. Or we can build, or architect, or code cyberspace to allow those values to disappear. There is no middle ground. There is no choice that does not include some kind of building. Code is never found; it is only ever made, and only ever made by us" (Lessig 2011:06).

Lessig's concerns are more legal than sociological. The values that Lessig speaks of are the values of free speech and openness. He is concerned that governments and corporations will want to remove the anonymity inherent in Internet usage and curtail the ability of users to manipulate information. But the importance of code in human behavior is cross-disciplinary. Because so many objects now use software in some form or other, an entire sub-discipline called software studies is developing around the premise that the software embedded in mundane objects is transforming everyday life (see Kitchin and Dodge 2011).

Within the context of this book, the most significant means through which code enables and constrains is by molding the types of social interaction within the digital environment. For example, social networking applications provide an ordered platform for people to organize relationships in the digital environment. This platform is only ever what is written through computer code. Consider the intuitive and visually appealing ways coders organize content for the users of their site—think about timeline on Facebook or circles on Google. These are nothing more than blocks of code.

An elegant study on the design of social networking sites, done by Sohn and Leckenby (2007), illustrate the power of code for molding human interaction. The researchers measured participation rates for two different designs of social networking sites. One design, a community board similar to the popular classified ad website Craigslist, allowed users to post to one general forum. A second design, a series of personally owned blogs connected to a central webpage similar to networking websites like Facebook, allowed users to post comments on their own private spaces. The authors found that the second design, personally owned blogs, generated more participant response than users who posted to a common community board.

Another study shows the power of code in enabling extremist attitudes. In *A Space for Hate,* Adam Klein (2009) writes about the white supremacist movement in the digital environment. Klein writes that one way in which white supremacists work to mobilize people who support the movement is by ginning up discontent through online forums. He calls this process message escalation. "For every statement made in a public forum" Klein writes, "numerous responses follow from other members resounding even louder themes of white-oppression, Jewish conspiracy, black violence, etc., until eventually aggressive action is suggested" (2009: 166). This polarization occurs because of the design of boards. The conversations on any given board is organized linearly, such that one person responds to the person who posted directly before her. When the majority of posters have similar views the overall tenor of the responses becomes more extreme over time. These discussions can be described as increasing in extremism monotonically. Views may stay at the same level of extremism for some time on the board. Eventually, however, someone will come along and present an idea that ratchets up the level of extremism. The conversation has then moved to a new, permanently higher level, where it may again stay at this level for some time before being ratcheted up again. Thus, a conversation may begin with, in what is a common theme on white supremacist websites, the belief that Jews are controlling aspects of the media. This idea will then be supported and commented on for some time, with little or no contrary arguments. Eventually, a user will make a more extreme claim. The user may say that not only are Jews controlling the media, but they are also using the media to control the lives of American citizens. This new more extreme claim now becomes the basis of support and comments. And so on.

For the social scientist, it is not necessary to understand a programming language in order to explore the social phenomena happening in the digital environment. But there needs to be a level of sensitivity to the way in which programming molds what we can and cannot do, similar to the way in which a scholar of the urban environment needs to be sensitive to state and federal policies that regulate neighborhoods and communities.

OTHER POSSIBLE PROPERTIES: SPEED AND QUANTITY OF INFORMATION

The properties above are the most important for describing the DE. They are broad enough so to engulf more narrow properties. There are other properties of the DE that could have also been included. Two that come to mind are speed of information, the quantity of information. I did not include these properties because, although they matter, they are not in my view as fundamental to understanding social interaction in the digital environment. They can either be subsumed under the properties already outlined, or have relatively less impact on social interaction. The quantity of information and the speed of information flow are clearly different in the DE than the PE. People entering into the DE have at their disposal a vast quantity of knowledge and the ability to transmit that knowledge nearly instantaneously. One can conclude that the vast quantity of information available is due to the fact, in Property 1, that information is easier to manipulate. Likewise, the use of the term propinquity in Property 3 assumes that time (thus speed) is not a factor in communication.

DIGITAL PRACTICES

When groups enter into the digital environment, they may need to modify their actions or adopt wholly new ones in order to make the space culturally meaningful and rewarding. I call these new or modified behaviors digital practices. A simple working definition of digital practices can be the behaviors that result when groups navigate the digital environment.

Although the DE is now a mature ecosystem, it has only been in the new millennium that groups down the class spectrum and across racial lines have been able to enjoy full access to it. Scholars have recognized—at least in Western countries—that access is no longer a problem, and have focused more on quality of usage because of this fact (see Chapter 2). And so groups in society are still working out the most efficient ways to use this space, and behaviors are still being routinized. The paragraphs that follow discuss ways in which we can think about these new or modified behaviors.

New Leverage for Old Behaviors

The Internet provides "new leverage for old behaviors" (Shirky 2008). People are using the technology available to them to accomplish their goals in life. All technology, from pick axes to nuclear warheads, can be leveraged, because of their particular properties or "affordances" (Hutchby 2001).

The notion of "new leverage for old behaviors" may require a few illustrations. Gershon (2012) found that a set of expectations have evolved around the use of Facebook for ending a relationship. The "old behavior", in this case, is ending a relationship, and the normative ways of doing so. The "new leverage" is Facebook, texting, and e-mail. When ending relationships, Gershon shows, people use a range of media to navigate the breakup. In some cases, a refusal to use a certain ICT presents a way of ensuring a breakup. For example one person may refuse to use voice, which is perceived as more intimate, and instead only communicate via e-mail, which can be seen as more formal. This is no different than a person screening their calls via answering machine and only communicating via snail mail or through a third party. E-mail provides new leverage for the old behaviors of splitting up.

A second example would be quite familiar to teachers. A popular argument in faculty lounges is that text messaging is eroding students' ability to communicate, and students cannot express themselves as well as they did in the past. But of course, teachers don't mean that students are walking around grunting and babbling incomprehensibly. They communicate just fine. What they surely mean is that text messaging has modified the norms of communication. Linguist Naomi Baron (2008) has taken up this issue, and after analyzing data from IM and text messages, writes that: "If you look at the effects—direct or otherwise—on traditional language, the case is highly tenuous....When it comes to speech, the potential effects of the Internet (at least as of now) are negligible at best" (180). Baron shows that text messaging, far from eroding speech or even changing it in any demonstrable way, is allowing a generation of speakers who are less concerned about the rules of language (old behavior) to produce new neologisms and abbreviations using IM and texting (new leverage).

Historically and Structurally Conditioned Goals

Above I give examples of college students and people going through breakups, showing how they leverage the DE to reach goals unique to their conditions. The same logic applies to the major dimensions of stratification in social science research—class, race, ethnicity, and gender. People of different classes, racial or ethnic groups, and genders also experience unique conditions.

The difference is one of magnitude. The person who is going through a breakup is experiencing one finite, circumscribed instance where her situation can lead to leveraging the properties of the DE in a certain way. However, people of different economic classes or different racial backgrounds *experience their entire lives in different ways*. This difference in experience is produced through historical factors and present structural factors.

Consider people of different class backgrounds. People from working class and middle class backgrounds grow up in different worlds, being taught different values, beliefs, and life expectation (Lareau 2003). This difference in socialization affects choices in entertainment, higher education, political views, gender roles, and so on. In this way, the class position of a person is a historical condition, and that person brings that history into every context, including when he or she enters the DE. That same person also has a present class position based upon his occupation. This occupation—its income, the degree of autonomy and control it offers, its meaningfulness—all produce current structural conditions that also affect every context, including when he or she enters the DE.

Consider someone with a working class background, who is currently employed in a working class occupation. Working class jobs often offer little autonomy or control over one's working conditions. People working in this type of job may be more likely to assert some freedom over their daily lives by using their mobile phones to enter the DE whenever possible. These are current structural conditions at play here. And so a study may show a "digital practice" that it is the working class security guard or dental assistant who is more active with his or her mobile device than the middle class lawyer or dentist. Furthermore, the choice in entertainment, the "taste" of the person, is affected by historical factors. Furthermore, that study may show differences in the choices of entertainment between groups, with each group gravitating to entertainment suited to their taste.

For me, the most interesting digital practices will always be those associated with economic classes, ethnoracial groups, and gender—particularly the categories within these groups that are disadvantaged. People who are poorer, racial minorities, and women have traditionally been disadvantaged in the physical environment. I think the historical and structural conditions these groups endure in the physical environment present an enormous incentive for these groups to be more aggressive in the digital environment.

Types of Digital Practices

There are at least three types of digital practices, and I discuss them below in order of increasing complexity. Table 3.4 summarizes these three types.

The first type of digital practice is the norms that develop and coalesce around a single technology in the DE. Access to the DE occurs through a particular technology, say a mobile application. The application itself is not as important, as it is only a conduit. However, a particular set of patterns arises around this application as people use it to interact in the DE in a specific manner. Each new technology can be considered "wild" and unknown. Groups learn how to "tame" these wild technologies and incorporate them into their daily lives.[4] Uncovering the norms surrounding a given type of technology is the most common type of social science work on ICTs, illustrated by research on social networking sites (Ellison et al. 2007, 2011), Twitter (Lassen and Brown 2010; Hargittai and Litt 2011) and so on. In my own work, I have written about the digital practices of mobile phones (Graham 2012). There I summarized research on mobile phone usage, and identified four digital practices that were common to users across the globe.

The second type of digital practice focuses on social groups, and what ways groups are interacting in the DE. The identification of this practice places technology in the background, and focuses more on the behavior of groups after they have used technology to enter into the DE.

Consider a research question such as: In what ways are visual artists promoting their art online? This question focuses on the cultural aspects of a group's usage of the DE. It assumes that a culture of presenting one's work has been routinized in the PE, and that these cultural patterns may be modified in the DE. If different behaviors are uncovered in the course of the research, then these behaviors can be understood as a digital practice of visual artists. This is a fictitious study, but one can imagine that visual artists have indeed leveraged the properties of the DE. It may be that they are incorporating photosharing sites into their repertoire of publicizing and social networking. Or, certain norms of interaction may develop. The community of visual artists may come to some agreement as to appropriate ways of sharing images. This second type of digital practice reveals significantly more about how social and cultural life has been changed in the Information Society. The work that I present in this book is aimed at this level of complexity.

A third type of digital practice focuses on the interplay between several groups in the DE, possibly with opposing structurally and historically conditioned desires. This practice can also be about the interplay between a social group and institutions that have reached into the DE. The practices identified here are sociological processes. Consider this research question: "Does online education reproduce or mitigate educational inequities between wealthy and poor students"? This question requires an understanding of (1) a digital practice associated with a technology—MOOCs[5] or an online course management system like Blackboard, (2) a digital practice associated with a group as they learn in the DE—wealthy and poor students use these technologies, and (3) how our educational system has been and may continue to be a source of inequality. To make clear the differences between the second type of digital practice, and this third, more complex type, I return to the example of artists and photo sharing. A study may reveal that photosharing allows working class artists who are attending less prestigious art schools to publicize their work more easily, lowering the gap in exposure between them and more wealthy students who tend to go to more prestigious art schools. This can lead to mitigation in the amount of inequality between those working class students who attend less prestigious schools and middle class students who have more access to top-tier schools. This third type of digital practice reveals the most about out Information Society. However, it is clearly the most methodologically demanding, requiring several studies over a period of time.

Table 3.4. Types of Digital Practices

Type of Practice	Description	Complexity
Social Processes in the DE	The changes in social processes as a result of several groups and institutions interacting in the DE	Most Complex
The Practices of Groups in the DE	The norms of interaction that are associated with a group using technology in the DE	
The Practice of Using a Technology	The norms associated with a technology	Least Complex

The topics in this book, as I will discuss below, all revolve around African Americans, and the questions I ask deal with what this group is doing in the DE. The answers to these questions may hint at the third level of digital practices, but mainly describe a second-level practice.

APPLYING A DIGITAL PRACTICE PERSPECTIVE

The digital practice perspective is not a theory per se. Instead, it is a different lens through which to view the Information Society. Looking through this lens allows a focus on the accomplishment of everyday tasks in the digital environment. Anyone can use some or all of the ideas to inform their understandings. Some may find the concept of the digital environment instructive, and its four properties appealing. Conversely, some may find the notion of digital practices useful in describing the unique patterns associated with ICTs, but feel no need to think of a separate space where these patterns are occurring. In the final analysis, if some or all of the ideas presented in this chapter help reveal the agency of people via ICTs in everyday life then the perspective has been useful.

In the chapters that follow, I will use the digital practice perspective to explore the behavior of African Americans. In using this perspective, I ask myself three basic questions. These questions are:

1. *What historical and current structural conditions are important?*
2. *How do the properties of the digital environment create the conditions for new practices (i.e., what leverage is available)?*
3. *Within which layer(s) is this leveraging occurring?*

The first question is meant to focus one's attention on the PE, and its influences. The second question does the same for the DE. The third question is meant to focus attention onto the technology at play, understanding that while it is ultimately the environment that matters, users still must interface through one of the layers of the DE. By answering all three questions, one applies the digital practice perspective fully.

CONCLUSION

Chapters 1 and 2 were about ways of seeing the Information Society that in my view were technologically and economically deterministic. The digital environment, or DE, is distinct from the physical environment, or PE. It is a space where one must enter into via ICTs. Upon entry, one is faced with a new set of social forces, the navigation of which requires adopting new behaviors. Digital practices, then, are the behaviors that result when groups navigate the digital environment. The use of these concepts, the ideas associated with them, and their implications amount to a "digital practice perspective". I used several examples throughout this chapter in an effort to explain these concepts, from the Mermaid Day Parade to young people texting to people in working class jobs. This was in an effort to exhibit the wide applicability of the digital practice perspective. In the chapters that follow, my focus will be squarely on African Americans and their exploits in the digital environment.

I chose African Americans for several reasons. First, African Americans presented a paradox for me. On the one hand, research has shown that African Americans have had lower levels of ICT access and skill (Mossberger et al 2003; Hargittai 2010). They were on the wrong side of the metaphorical digital divide. On the other hand, my everyday experiences and personal research (Graham 2010, Graham and Smith 2010) did not jibe with the narrative that African Americans were "have nots". They seemed to be extracting a lot of benefits from ICTs. I needed to resolve this contradiction. Second, African Americans, as a population, are ideal for studying how groups leverage the properties of the DE. Relative to other groups, it is easier for me to identify the historically and structurally contingent factors that lead to digital practices.

But I can find these first two reasons in other groups. For example, Hispanics also present a paradox. They are also assumed to be "have nots", but recent research paints a more complex picture. Or, Jewish Americans have managed to maintain their distinctiveness to a degree greater than other European groups and one can point to historical and structural factors with that group also. The third reason, and main one, is because I am African American. I am inherently interested in the technological exploits of African Americans and what this means for racial equality in the United States.

It may be a bit dramatic to say that the digital environment will be the main site in the battle for racial inequality in the 21st century, but clearly differences between racial groups can be exacerbated or mitigated depending upon differential leveraging of the DE. The nation's focus, when racial inequality and technology are concerned, is usually economic, focusing on the consumption of ICTs or contributing to the production of ICTs: Can minorities purchase technology at the same rates as whites (read: are they consuming technology)? Are minorities entering into tech fields as much as whites (read: are they producing technology)? These are clearly important questions, but questions about noneconomic phenomena also need to be asked. This will be the purpose of the next several chapters.

CHAPTER FOUR

The Digital Practice of Weak Tie Development

INTRODUCTION

In this chapter I apply the digital practice perspective to African Americans and social networking. The research I present was done with my colleague, Dr. Danielle Smith from the Rochester Institute of Technology. This research illustrates a way in which African Americans take advantage of the properties of the digital environment. African Americans use social networking sites significantly more than other racial groups to build contacts with others who are not a part of their social circle. This is a digital practice of African Americans.

This desire to use the digital environment in this way is borne out of historical and structural conditions in the physical environment. Historically, one of the defining characteristics of African American family and social life has been helping each other. While African Americans are keen to follow normalized routes to success, they have experienced enough racism and discrimination to understand that sometimes one needs to go outside of established routes to reach one's goals. And so throughout their history, African Americans have given and relied upon assistance from others—usually those closest to them—to achieve their ends. They understand the need for connections. Structurally, African Americans are more segregated than other racial groups. They tend to live in segregated neighborhoods more, intermarry less, and experience more segregation in public spaces. These historical and structural conditions, Dr. Smith and I argue, provide African Americans with a unique set of cultural tools and a real necessity to leverage them. We found that African Americans, more than other groups, use social networking sites to connect with people outside of their immediate circles. We suggest that this is an attempt to redress the structural segregation found in the physical environment.

The research that went into writing this chapter was done before my thinking had coalesced around notions of a digital environment and digital practices. But these findings hinted at something new. Here was an example of a phenomenon that could not be neatly understood by using Information Society models or digital divide metaphors. There were two worlds. One world—of brick and mortar and metal—had segregated African Americans. But here was a new world, made of bits and bytes. It was a distinct environment possessing a new suite of properties. And here were African Americans exhibiting a different practice in this new environment.

SOCIAL CAPITAL AND SOCIAL NETWORKS

A good working definition of social capital can be the resources one has access to through one's relationship with others (Bourdieu 1985, Coleman 1988, Burt 1995). People with more social capital are able to get help when they need it. They can call on people who can provide money, information, or just their labor. From our own everyday experiences, we know that some people are in a better position to get that job, get help with that research paper, get a good babysitter, and so on because of the people they know. Social capital is, on balance, a good thing to have.[1] Social capital does not reside in the person themselves, but instead the networks that a person is enmeshed in or connections she has. Princeton sociologist Alejandro Portes (1998) writes that "To possess social capital, a person must be related to others, and it is those others, not himself, who is the actual source of his or her advantage" (p. 7).

Social scientists call the connection between you and another person a "tie". There are two types of ties, or ways in which you can be connected to another person. One way is through a "strong" tie. Family, significant others, and close friends generally are connected by strong ties. People whom we have met at, say, a church or a local hangout, and can also be considered as a strong tie if we have developed a history with that person. A strong tie is based on an emotional connection with a person. It is called "strong" because these ties are durable and traverse many domains of life and remain active over a long period of time. Family members stay with us from birth till death, lovers become fully integrated into our lives, and some of us keep friends we met in grade school throughout our entire lives. Because of the nature of strong ties it is usually the case that people connected by these ties share socioeconomic characteristics and tend to be of the same race, religion, or class.

The social capital generated through strong ties is called "bonding" capital. Generally speaking, African Americans tend to have a good deal of bonding capital and can rely on their family and extended kin networks to provide support.

Another way that people can be connected is through a "weak" tie. Weak ties are connections you have with people whom you may not be particularly close to but you recognize and are friendly with. Maybe you spend time at the same coffee shop, or you work together and exchange niceties on the elevator. Or maybe you are taking a class with that person. A connection via a weak tie is often based on task—work, school, etc. And, as the label weak implies, the connection is easily broken: when that task is over, so is the relationship. People connected through weak ties tend to be more diverse (heterogeneous) than people connected through strong ties. The people who happen to order coffee at the same time as you, or work on the same floor as you may not be similar to you in social background. The type of social capital generated through these connections can be called "bridging" capital primarily because the capital is produced through a bridge across social groups. African Americans, as I will discuss later, tend to have far less bridging capital than whites.

So, there are two types of social capital—bonding capital and bridging capital. They are generated through two different types of relationships with others. Bonding capital is generated through strong ties: long lasting, intimate connections with family and friends. Bridging capital is generated through weak ties: less permanent, task-oriented connections with co-workers, people you routinely share a bus ride with, fellow students in a class, and other casual acquaintances.

The Strength of Weak Ties

While weak ties are less durable than strong ones, the bridging capital produced in them can be very important. They can give you access to information not currently available to you: even if you have numerous strong ties and a wealth of bridging capital. Because the people who share strong ties tend to be homogenous, their general understandings—values, beliefs, symbolic meanings—may also be quite similar. Imagine that you and your friends are making a decision about going to a movie. If your friends are under 40 and African American, it is a good bet that seeing the latest Tyler Perry film would be at or near the top of their must see list. If it is not at the top, it is almost certain that they know of the movie and would not be surprised if the suggestion to go see it is made. However, my guess is that no one in that group would suggest the latest Werner Herzog film. No matter how critically acclaimed that director is, this option is not available simply because it is unknown. Information is redundant between you and the people you share strong ties with. Strong ties are vital for accomplishing most aspects of everyday life–there will be no problem with you and your friends picking a movie you can all agree on and go and enjoy. But they are less effective at providing new perspectives and new opportunities.

Sociologist Mark Granovetter (1973) observed that the strength of one's weak ties can be vital to social mobility. Individuals with expansive social networks, connecting them to many different types of people, have the ability to tap into varied pools of information. African Americans tend to have less expansive social networks than whites. The example I used above may not make clear that having bridging capital can be a boon to social mobility. But weak ties don't just help with thinking outside of the box for movie choices. One can gain information that can better one's socioeconomic situation as well. The most obvious example is job leads. But information about new certificate programs at a local community college is also an avenue to social mobility. Many people, especially working adults with families, may find it impossible to invest the time and cost of two years in a college (and usually more if one is attending part-time). However, many colleges and non-profits offer certificate programs that can be completed in months. This type of knowledge about opportunities within the educational system can be passed through weak ties. Another example can be civic knowledge. How to take advantage of programs offered by government agencies can also lead to social mobility. Understanding how to take advantage of changes in the tax code or understanding one's eligibility for loan forgiveness programs can be worth hundreds or even thousands of dollars.

Scholars have pointed out repeatedly that African Americans are network disadvantaged with respect to weak ties and bridging capital (Elliot 1999, Loury 1977, Parks-Yancy et al. 2009, Peterson et al., 2000, Rankin and Quane 2000, Tigges et al. 1988, Wilson 1987). This means that their chances of meeting someone who can provide them information for a new job opportunity or some other unique piece of information are comparatively less. This is true for many groups in society. Compared to whites, non-white groups (Erickson 2004, Moren-Cross and Lin 2008) and immigrants (Behtoui and Neergaard 2010) have less varied social networks and less of the type of bridging capital that can lead to jobs.

This is especially acute, however, for African Americans. At least one of the explanations for this is the high levels of residential and social segregation African Americans must tolerate. We have images of poor African Americans living in blighted inner-city neighborhoods. But even for the growing African American middle class, research shows that they live in neighborhoods that are heavily black and are more likely to be populated not with other people of the middle class but people from the working class (Massey and Denton 1993, Quillan 1999, Fischer et al. 2004). While working class families make fine neighbors, they may not be able to provide the type of information that can advance the careers of many middle class professionals. Thus even African Americans in white collar settings (Ibarra 1995) and those attempting to start their own businesses (Harvey 2005) have comparatively fewer connections compared to whites.

STRONG TIES AND THE "HOOK-UP" IN THE AFRICAN AMERICAN COMMUNITY

African Americans have a dearth of weak ties, but a wealth of strong ties. African Americans help each other out. Within the circle of nuclear family members, extended kin, and family friends, help is asked for and given frequently. The person asking for help is not seen as morally deficient, nor is the person giving it seen as superior. Unless that person makes repeated overtures for help and rarely reciprocates, someone's asking for and getting help is not only tolerated but *expected*.

Carol Stack (1974) wrote in *All Our Kin*, "The black urban family, embedded in cooperative domestic exchange, proves to be an organized tenacious, active, lifelong, network" (124). Stack's work was in some ways a response to the notion that African American families were dysfunctional. Spurred on by the enormously influential Moynihan report (1965), many of society's leaders were concerned that the structure of African American families, many of which were single parent and female headed, were dysfunctional. These families were judged to be incapable of providing the necessary emotional stability and economic security needed to raise children into productive adults. The high rates of crime, teen pregnancies, and high school dropout for African Americans were attributed to the dysfunctional African American family. Stack's work, and others like it, attempted to show that the composition and cultural patterns of the African American family were not the cause of poverty, crime, unemployment but in fact a response to it (Hill 1999). Stack writes that: "these highly adaptive structural features of urban black families comprise a resilient response to the social-economic conditions of poverty, [and] the inexorable unemployment of black women and men...." (124)

More recent research shows that Stack's observations in the 1970s are still relevant today (Cantor et al. 1994, Johnson and Barer 1990). To be sure, both white and African American families support their kin. However African American families tend to focus a bit more on practical, material support (Sarkisian and Gerstel 2004). In 2004, researchers from the University of Illinois published results from a series of interviews with poor, single parent African American mothers and their family members (McCreary and Dancy 2004). The purpose of the research was to understand how these families functioned. From the interviews given, the researchers saw how prevalent reciprocal exchanges were within the family. Here are the words of the respondents as quoted by the researchers (McCreary and Dancy 2004: 695):

- Child-care: "When I get off work, she be going to work, and I would take her daughter home [from school], pick up mine from day care, and keep 'em until she get home from work."
- Finance: "If someone is down and out, we try to help them out. Anytime we are in need, we always be there... like if you need a bill to be paid."
- Sharing food: "We pitch in when we can help. My mom might be short of food, can't buy groceries, you know, so I take a bag."

Giving and receiving help extends into relationships with other African American friends, co-workers, and acquaintances. When navigating environments outside of the family unit, African Americans are more likely to associate with other African Americans for the sole reason that they share a racial identity.[2] Coalitions are formed. Friendships are made. And then resources are shared. Adia Harvey (2006) writes about the "helping ideology" she observed in African American beauty salons. The women owners of these salons would provide a helping hand to other African American women by acting as mentors:

"The relationship between owners and stylists is unique in a number of respects. Possibly most striking is the ideology of help and support that shapes, to varying degrees, owners' relationships with stylists. Owners generally profess a willingness to assist stylists in their professional development and growth as well as a readiness to help them succeed in the business. In its most extreme cases, this helping ideology motivates owners to encourage stylists to pursue entrepreneurship and to open their own salons" (799–800).

Harvey writes about the relationship between one owner and stylist:

"Tanisha and Lana first met at church, and after learning that Tanisha styled hair for several of the women in the congregation, Lana decided to take Tanisha under her wing. Tanisha began working full-time for Lana immediately after high school and remained at this salon for three years before moving on to open her own salon" (p. 800).

This practice of African Americans giving help to each other, both to family members as well as acquaintances, is often termed colloquially *"hooking someone up"*. This means providing information to someone to spur economic mobility.[3] In this way, hooking someone up can mean anything from putting a good word in at a job, charging less for a service, or simply going out of one's way to help someone. Often, when someone gets a "hook up" they are provided with a means of working normal routes of attainment because those routes are riddled with racism and discrimination.

SOCIAL NETWORKING SITES

One of the properties of the digital environment is that networks are ahistorical and multidimensional (see Chapter 3). One way in which African Americans can access this property of the DE is through social networking sites. Social networking sites (SNSs) are "web-based services that allow individuals to (1) construct a public or semi-public profile within a bounded system, (2) articulate a list of other users with whom they share a connection, and (3) view and traverse their list of connections and those made by others within the system" (Boyd & Ellison, 2007, p. 211). The most popular social networking site is clearly Facebook with upwards of 800 million users at the time of this writing. However there are numerous SNSs including MySpace, LinkedIn, LiveJournal, Pinterest, Quora, and Google+.

In the early days of the Internet there was some initial concern that spending time online reduced one's connection with people (Nie 2001). However, most current research leads to the opposite conclusion. By and large the Internet reinforces strong ties by allowing close friends and family to communicate more, and increases the number of weak ties by allowing people to connect with others across space and time (Hampton and Wellman 2003, Benkler 2007). Using social networking sites will generally enhance, not diminish, one's connections to others.

For example, social scientists from Michigan State have done a series of studies exploring the relationship between Facebook use and social capital.[4] In 2008 they published a two-year study of college students who use Facebook (Steinfield et al. 2008). The study showed that intensity of Facebook use in year one was associated with an increase in bridging capital in year two. For this study bridging capital outcomes were measured by positive responses to questions such as "I am interested in what goes on at MSU" and "I feel I am a part of the MSU community". Interestingly, the biggest gains in bridging capital occurred with students who reported low levels of self-esteem. This suggests that the DE can counteract some of the barriers present in the PE. Having low self-esteem makes it difficult to initiate contact with others offline, but online environments make it easier to pick contexts and interactions where one's lack of self-esteem is less of an issue.

A later study looked at the effects of a social networking site within an organization (Steinfield et al. 2009). The study was done on an in-house social networking site created by a large multinational organization, only for its employees. Like the Facebook study done a year earlier, the researchers came to similar conclusions about the benefits of SNSs. They found that employees who used the SNS had more productive weak ties (in the sense that respondents feel more able to access information when needed). They also found that the benefits gained were greater for newer employees, younger employees, and employees working further away from the company's headquarters. This shows that SNS usage can help those who are structurally disadvantaged.

A third study from this group of researchers, again using students at Michigan State, asked the question: Do different ways of interacting on Facebook lead to differences in perceptions of social capital? (Ellison et al. 2011) Three strategies for interaction on Facebook were identified: (1) "initiating", or using Facebook to meet totally new people; (2) "information seeking", or using Facebook to learn more about a person whom the respondent recognizes from a dorm room or from a prior class; and (3) "maintaining", or using Facebook to communicate with people the respondent knows very well. As in previous studies, the research shows that Facebook has a positive effect on social capital. This study provided additional nuance. More positive responses were given to social capital questions for those students who did more "information seeking". Thus, Facebook can help convert latent ties into weak ties, but this is more so if there is already an offline connection—in this case attending the same university or living in the same dorm room. This study reinforces the idea that SNS can connect people if there is a basis for the connection.

The three studies conducted out of Michigan State show that the use of SNS generally increases social capital. This relationship appears to be the strongest with respect to weak tie development and the accumulation of bridging capital.

THE DIGITAL PRACTICE OF PURSUING BRIDGING CAPITAL THROUGH SOCIAL NETWORKING SITES

We arrive at this idea: The digital environment presents an opportunity for African Americans to network across class and racial lines. Social networking sites allow African Americans to develop networks that are ahistorical in that they can connect with people who they normally would not or could not. We expect African Americans to exhibit a particular pattern, or digital practice, on SNSs. African Americans will be avid "bridgers". Conversely, because of the strong ties evidenced within the African American community, we expect they will be less than enthusiastic "bonders"—or at any rate equal to the population at large.

I and a colleague of mine, Danielle Smith at the Rochester Institute of Technology, were able to explore these ideas with data collected from the Pew Internet and American Life project (Pew Internet and American Life 2008). This particular survey asked questions about the number of social networking sites a respondent participated in, and what types of activities they did while on these sites. With the answers to these questions, we could judge to what extent African Americans use social networking sites to develop weak ties and increase bridging capital. Our study was ordered by two hypotheses based on what we know about bridging, bonding, and African Americans:

1. Compared to whites[5], being African American will not be associated with an increase or decrease in bonding activities on social networking sites (alternatively, there will be no relationship between bonding and being African American).
2. Compared to whites, being African American will be associated with more bridging activities on social networking sites.

DATA

We used nationally representative data to examine differences between African Americans and other ethnoracial groups. The data for this research comes from the Pew Internet and American Life's "Spring Tracking Survey 2008" (Pew Internet and American Life 2008).[6]

Dependent Variables

The Pew survey asks respondents several questions that were related to social networking activity (Table 4.1). We have categorized most of these questions into indicators of "bonding" and "bridging". One question could not be easily categorized into one of these two categories. However, this question adds to our understanding of African American social networking activities, and it was included in the analysis as well.

Bonding. We measured bonding in four ways. First, we assessed site ownership, which measured whether or not a respondent reported currently having a profile on an SNS. We consider simply having a profile a measure of bonding. Our rationale is that above all else, the primary function of SNSs is bonding. Our sentiments converge with Mesch (2012), who argues:

> "Whereas chat rooms and forums are technologies that link individuals around a shared topic of interest and concern, SNSs are technologies that link individuals who have some knowledge of each other and belong to the same social circle or to the social circle of their friends.... Given these features of channels of communication, it is reasonable to expect that the motivation for the use of chat rooms and weblogs is to expand social ties and the use of SNSs to conserve existing ties" (323).

Thus, because the primary function of an SNS is to bond, the initial impetus to have a profile on a site may primarily be to bond with friends who also have joined the given site.

Table 4.1. Descriptive Statistics for Dependent Variables (% in Parentheses)

	N	No	Yes
Bonding			
Do you own an SNS profile?	2251	1913 (85)	338 (15)
Stay in Touch with Friends?	326	43 (13.2)	283 (86.8)
Make Plans with Your Friends?	327	150 (45.9)	177 (54.1)
Make New Friends?	328	157 (51.8)	326 (48.2)
Do You Flirt with Someone?	322	258 (80.1)	64 (19.9)
Bridging			
Do you own more than one SNS profile?	314	175 (55.7)	139 (44.3)
Make New Business and Professional Contacts?	326	233 (71.5)	93 (28.5)
Promote Yourself or Your Work?	327	237 (72.5)	90 (27.5)

Our next four measures focused on specific activities meant to develop strong or affective ties. These were: "*Do you stay in touch with friends?*", "*Do you make plans with your friends?*", "*Do you make new friends?*", and "*Do you flirt with someone?*" These activities, with their explicit references to friendship, connote the establishment of strong ties. These are bridging activities.

Bridging. We measured bridging in three ways. First, we measured whether or not a respondent reported owning an SNS site. Our rationale for including this as a bridging measure was that if one's purpose is to bond, then one site should be enough to maintain relationships with people you share strong ties with. This type of practice conforms to the prevailing notion of what a social networking site should be—one community where you and your friends can stay in touch. But, if a person joins several social networking sites, it suggests, albeit indirectly, that this person is searching for unique pools of information, and not just to maintain contact with people they already know. For example, a site like Facebook may be wholly sufficient for one's close friends and family (strong ties). However, one may also feel the need to expand one's contacts professionally, in which case joining a professional website like LinkedIn may be in order. Further, and this may be the case for minorities more than whites, certain sites cater to users who identify with their ethnic or racial background, such as Blackplanet.com or MiGente.com. A user may find more co-ethnics and more culturally relevant content on sites such as these than on generalist sites like Facebook or MySpace. Our final two measures for bridging activity were: "*Do you make new business or professional contacts*", and "*Do you promote yourself or your work?*" Given the professional, instrumental nature of these activities, they are rather clear attempts at developing weak ties.

Independent Variables

The independent variables for the analyses represent standard demographic and socioeconomic predictors and are presented in Table 4.2 below. We included "class" variables, income and education. We also included gender and age. These variables, which can be subsumed under the label of "digital divide" variables, have all been recognized to significantly affect Internet usage. Ultimately, all but the variable ethnoracial status is treated as a control. We expect that these controls will influence bonding and bridging, but we are primarily interested in ethnoracial differences.

Table 4.2. Univariate Statistics for Independent Variables

Variable	Frequency	Variable	Frequency
Education		Ethnoracial Status	
(N = 2220)		(N = 2191)	
Less than High School	8.9	White	81.8
High School	32.3	African American	9.8
Some College	26.0	Hispanic	4.8
College Graduate	32.7	Other	3.6
Income		Gender	
(N = 1755)			
Less than $20,000	17.2	Male	45.5
Between $20,000 and $40,000	24.2	Female	54.5
Between $40,000 and $100,000	41.2		
Over $100,000	17.5		

Continuous Variables		
	Mean	SD
Age	55.1	19.48

METHODS

Because all dependent variables are presented as "yes" or "no" questions, such that 1 = yes, and 0 = no[7], we used binary logistic regression to determine the net effect of being African American on social networking activity. One measure is ordinal—how many sites does the respondent have profiles on—but given the bi-modal distribution of this variable (not shown) we chose to recode it as dichotomous. For each variable, we present the odds ratio of being in one category of the dependent variable (coded 1) as opposed to being in the other category (coded 0).

RESULTS

Bonding

Measuring bonding allows for a test of the hypothesis that, compared to whites, being African American will not be associated with an increase or decrease in bonding activities on social networking sites. Results are shown in Table 4.3.

Table 4.3. Binary Logistic Regressions for Bonding Measures

Variable	Own SNS Profile? Odds-Ratio	Stay in Touch with Friends? Odds-Ratio	Make Plans with Friends? Odds-Ratio	Make New Friends? Odds-Ratio	Flirt? Odds-Ratio
Age	.915***	.947***	.971***	.997	.989
Female	1.29***	1.47	.931	.612***	.236***
Income[1]					
Less than $20,000	1.48***	1.17	1.13	1.98***	1.45
Between $20,000 and $40,000	.989	2.18*	.469***	.705*	.536**
Over $100,000	.835	.450**	.739	.346***	.307***
Education[2]					
Less than High School	1.52***	3.01**	1.17	1.16	1.31
Some College	2.11***	10.02***	2.05***	.748	1.14
College Graduate	1.96***	1.05	.343***	.429***	.486**
Ethnoracial Status[3]					
White	1.32*	1.80	.845	.875	.519**
Hispanic	1.73***	1.41	.883	.998	1.41
Other	1.73**	.811	.250***	.427**	.326**
Constant	4.28	22.58	5.97***	2.56***	1.37
Nagelkerke R^2	.359	.294	.241	.153	.200
N	1553	326	327	328	322

*p<.05, **p<.01, ***p<.001
1—Between $40,000 and $100,0000 as Reference Category
2—High School as Reference Category
3—African American as Reference Category

Own an SNS Profile? Older respondents are less likely to own an SNS profile—a year increase in age is associated with .085% decrease in odds of owning an SNS profile. Females are more likely to own an SNS profile, with the odds of a woman owning an SNS profile 29% greater than the odds of a male owning a profile. There is not much difference in income groupings, although respondents in poverty are more likely to own an SNS profile than respondents making between $40,000 and $100,000. Turning our attention to race and ethnicity, we see that African Americans are less likely to report owning an SNS than whites. Specifically, the odds of a white respondent reporting that they own an SNS profile is 32% more than the odds of an African American reporting that they own an SNS profile. African Americans are also less likely to report owning an SNS than other ethnoracial groups. The odds of both Hispanics and other ethnoracial groups are 73% greater than for African American respondents.

Bonding Activities. We measured four bonding activities—staying in touch with friends, making plans with friends, making new friends, and flirting. Looking at control variables, we see that for most variables older respondents are less likely to report doing bonding activities. We see that middle income respondents, those making between $40,000 and $100,000 are in general more likely to report doing bonding activities, with the exception being when compared to those making less than $20,000. As far as education, there is no clear pattern. We can say that those with less than a high school diploma and those with some college are more likely to do bonding activities while those with a college degree are less likely to do bonding activities.

Looking at bonding activities, we see that there is very little difference between African Americans and whites, or African Americans and Hispanics. However, respondents who are not one of the three major ethnoracial categories are doing less bonding than African Americans. They are 75% less likely to make plans with friends, 57% less likely to make new friends, and 67% less likely to flirt than African Americans.

Bridging

Measuring bridging allows us to test the hypothesis that, compared to whites, being African American will be associated with more bridging activities on SNSs. Results are shown in Table 4.4.

Owing Multiple SNS Profiles. Age was again negatively associated with this measure. Gender was also significant, as females were 45% less likely than males to own multiple profiles. Income is significantly associated with this measure. However, this association is not consistent. Those in the lowest income category (less than $20,000) are more likely than the reference group (between $40,000 and $100,000) to own multiple profiles, but respondents in the next highest income category are less likely than the reference group. Both of these categories are lower income than the reference category, and thus one cannot summarize and say that income has a positive or negative effect based on this data. Education has very little association, with only high school respondents reporting significant levels of owning more than one profile than the reference category.

Table 4.4. Binary Logistic Regressions for Bridging Measures

Variable	More than One Profile	Make New Business Contacts	Promote Yourself
	Odds-Ratio	Odds-Ratio	Odds-Ratio
Age	.989*	1.02***	1.01*
Female	.546***	.357***	.355***
Income[1]			
Less than $20,000	1.70**	.667*	.584**
Between $20,000 and $40,000	.446***	.786	.828
Over $100,000	.444***	1.05	.885
Education[2]			
Less than High School	.518**	.882	2.11***
Some College	.969	1.26	1.14
College Graduate	1.07	1.35	1.21
Ethnoracial Status[3]			
White	.585**	.265***	.279***
Hispanic	.620*	.387***	.480**
Other	.711	.130***	.418**
Constant	3.11***	.994	1.11
Nagelkerke R^2	.102	.134	.120
N	314	326	317

*p<.05, **p<.01, ***p<.001
1—Between $40,000 and $100,0000 as Reference Category
2—High School as Reference Category
3—African American as Reference Category

For race and ethnicity, we see that African Americans are 41% more likely than whites to report owning more than one profile. They are also 38% more likely than Hispanics to report owning more than one profile.

Bridging Activities. For bridging activities, making new business contacts and promoting yourself or your work, there are three clear patterns. Contrary to other measures, Age is positively related. This is, in all likelihood because as one gets older one's career becomes more paramount in one's life. Second, males are more likely to report doing bridging activities. Females are 64% less likely to make new business contacts and promote themselves or their work. Third, the "class" variables of income and education have little effect on bridging activities, compared to bonding activities.

We see clear patterns with respect to race and ethnicity as well. All ethnoracial groups are less likely to report doing bridging activities than African Americans. Looking at whites, we see that the odds of a white respondent reporting making new business contacts is 74% less than the odds of an African American respondent, and the odds of a white respondent reporting that they promoted themselves or their work was 72% less than the odds of an African American doing so.

SUMMARY OF FINDINGS

Hypothesis 1 was that compared to whites, being African American will not be associated with an increase or decrease in bonding activities on social networking sites. We see enough evidence to support this hypothesis with qualifications. In most cases there are no significant differences between African Americans and whites. But, African Americans were more likely to flirt on social networking sites than whites, and less likely to own a profile than whites. Hypothesis 2 was that compared to whites, being African American will be associated with more bridging activities on social networking sites. We measured bonding through "promoting yourself at work", "making business contacts", and "owning more than one profile". This hypothesis was strongly supported. For all three of these measures, being African American was associated with an increased likelihood over whites and other ethnoracial groups.

In sum, African Americans are "bridgers" on social networking sites. We can say that this networking behavior is a digital practice for African Americans. The explanation we have for this bridging is that, due to the structural and historical conditions that African Americans experience in the physical environment (higher levels of social isolation and a cultural precedent of giving and receiving practical support) African Americans leverage the properties of the DE (ahistorical and multidimensional networks) to build weak ties. To be sure, there are no guarantees that attempts at developing weak ties lead to actual gains in bridging capital. Other research is needed to see, for example, if African Americans are more likely than whites to report that they got their job lead through an online source. If scholars find out that the efforts at developing weak ties are not realized, it does not invalidate the argument. Instead, the next step for scholars would be to understand how to direct or supplement this digital practice so that it can generate more connections and more social mobility.

CONCLUSION

This research was done before my ideas about digital environments and digital practices had materialized. But the findings screamed for a different understanding. Within the Information Society literature, networking is one of the dominant themes. But networking is always discussed within a technological context (e.g., Facebook makes it easier to connect) or within an economic context (e.g., corporations can spread across the globe because they are networked). But for these findings, a better explanation is one that relies on cultural context and meaning making. Similarly, digital divide models would lead one to an opposite conclusion to what we found. An application of the digital divide metaphor would suggest that African Americans would be supremely disadvantaged and unable to use technology to their advantage. In fact what we see is that African Americans are quite savvy navigators of the digital environment, so much so that within the context of using social networking sites to at least *attempt* to bridge, they are the "haves" and other groups are the "have nots".

CHAPTER FIVE

The Digital Practice of Maintaining Family Ties via Mobile Phone

INTRODUCTION

Chapter 4 presented work that predated notions of the digital environment and digital practices. In this chapter, I will present a case study that was derived directly from the application of the digital practice perspective. The study's impetus was a finding from a Pew Research Center's Internet & American Life Project report. The report, entitled "Mobile Access 2010"[1], said that minorities were more mobile than whites:

> "Continuing a trend we first identified in 2009, minority Americans lead the way when it comes to mobile access…minority Americans are significantly more likely to own a cell [mobile] phone than their white counterparts (87% of blacks and Hispanics own a cell phone, compared with 80% of whites). Additionally, black and Latino cell phone owners take advantage of a much wider array of their phones' data functions compared to white cell phone owners" (Smith 2010).

For the casual observer these findings do not converge with common understandings of who are the most mobile and tech savvy people in society. The young, the white, and the male are seen as those that should be at the vanguard in the adoption and use of technology. Hispanics and blacks are understood, in this narrative, to be lagging behind. This understanding holds true for social scientists as well. Social science research has operated under the assumption—not wholly unwarranted—that minorities are disadvantaged with respect to the acquisition and usage of information and communication technologies (see Chapter 2). But the Pew report's conclusions are derived from good survey data that represent the American population. There is something to this idea that minorities are more mobile than whites. So why do mobile phones deviate from our common understandings?

The answer may lie in the everyday uses of mobile phones for minorities. One possible reason for the differences between whites and minorities are the different levels of complexity in family structures and the corresponding differences in communication needed to maintain cohesion. Social scientists have produced a wealth of research showing that a primary function of the mobile phone is to maintain contact with family. Non-whites, and especially African Americans, have more people who are considered close family to take into account, and stronger cultural expectations to maintain emotional contact with those family members. The digital environment, via the hardware of mobile phones, provides a new leverage for non-whites to continue the old behavior of maintaining contact with family members.

APPLYING A DIGITAL PRACTICE PERSPECTIVE

The idea that differences in mobile phone use can be explained by differences in family structures is in line with a digital practice perspective. The meanings attached to family communication and mobile phone uses are simply different for whites and African Americans. If we wish to apply the digital practice perspective more systematically, we must ask and answer three questions:

1. *What historical and current structural conditions are important?* African Americans have diverse family structures. As I will explain in more detail below, research suggests that they construct more expansive kin networks, and they must keep in contact with clusters of these extended kin in different parts of the country. This is a current structural condition. Historically, African Americans have exhibited cultural patterns that allow these types of families to function quite well: from fathers who do not live with their children managing to be a part of their children's lives, to a general helping ideology applied to all family members, to the routinized trips from North to South for clusters of families who moved during the Great Migration. These points will be expanded in more detail below.

2. *How do the properties of the digital environment create the conditions for new practices (i.e., what leverage is available)?* The digital environment by its

very nature allows for communication without regard for space and time—community without propinquity. This is the third property of the digital environment, and is most important here. Networked individualism, a concept I will discuss in more detail below, is at its core the ability of individuals to maintain connections with others despite not sharing a physical space with them. The mobile phone makes this easier. Because of the portability and size of the mobile phone, context is less of a barrier to entry and people can enjoy the benefits of the DE more often.

3. *Within which layer(s) is this leveraging occurring?* As with any study, there are several ways to approach the topic of family structure. The layers that I consider most important are the hardware and human layers. The design of the mobile phone—portable and relatively inconspicuous—is the prime reason why the mobile phone can break so many contextual barriers. A study of the way in which the mobile phone is carried on a person's body or integrated into a person's home or office can reveal much about the breaking of these contextual barriers. A second level, the human level is also significant here. The density of African American familial networks combined with the cultural expectations of maintaining them present a powerful incentive to be more mobile. I will focus on this layer.

The three questions and answers above provide a quick sketch of the rationale for the study. I expound on these ideas below.

NETWORKED INDIVIDUALISM WITHIN FAMILIES

Castells et al. (2006) write: "As contemporary families often exist as micro-distributive networks across multiple sites with translocal and sometimes transnational reach, mobile technologies have been widely adopted in the family setting throughout the world" (p. 87). In plain speak: family members are using mobile phones to keep in contact with each other across space and time. They go on to say that "an unprecedented phenomenon has emerged that almost all family members of a large number of households are networked at all times" (p. 89).

Yes. The use of the mobile phone by family members is extensive, pervasive, and global. As such, it has been studied extensively (Katz and Aakhus 2002; Horst and Miller 2006; Donner 2007; Ling 2008a, 2008b; Yang 2008). One of the more useful conceptual approaches to understanding this phenomenon is that of "networked individualism" popularized by Barry Wellman (Kennedy and Wellman 2007; Rainie and Wellman 2012). Networked individualism describes the move away from networks as static and rooted in the physical environment, to more fluid, personalized networks rooted in the digital environment. People are no longer moored to the groups that they share physical space with—one does not need to only interact with one's neighbors, extended family, or co-workers. In today's society, people have more control over their social networks. They are interacting through a battery of ICTs with a diverse set of individuals.

In *Networked: The New Social Operating System*, Lee Rainie, director of the Pew research center's Internet and American Life Project, and Wellman (2012) use a wealth of data to discuss how networked individuals operate in their personal, family, and work lives. For this chapter, of special interest is how this idea of networked individualism applies to the family:

> "Networked families...use ICTs to bridge barriers of time and space, weakening the boundaries between public and private life spaces. The mounting and interrelated changes in the composition of households—such as the life-cycle complexities of marriage and divorce and decisions to have children—mean that today's households are varied, complex, and evolving. Networked families use ICTs to mediate these complexities and adapt ICTs to their varied needs" (Wellman and Rainie 2012: 170).

Rainie and Wellman chronicle the many ways in which family life has changed as ICTs have been embraced. Families have reorganized their homes to accommodate ICTs, with computers placed in communal spaces. As families grow larger they buy more ICTs to allow more access to members. Spouses organize their tasks and errands using ICTs, in particular mobile phones. Parents have embraced ICTs, again in particular the mobile phone, as a way to parent from afar.

The use of ICTs within a family context is in large part a response to structural changes in how a family is now constructed. The modern family has a new look in the 21st century. There are fewer families whose composition would be considered "traditional"—co-residing parents with biologically related children. The biggest change is the rise of single mothers. However, there are also more people cohabitating or living with new spouses who have children from previous relationships. Furthermore, the move of women into the workforce has changed family dynamics. In some cases, fathers have become more involved in parenting. In other cases, when there is no involvement from the father, women must try and juggle work and childcare alone. These changes in family structure mean a moving from a more static routine of mother anchoring the home and handling home duties until father gets home, to a more dynamic situation in which one or both parents must juggle parenting in between work obligations.

THE UNIQUENESS OF MOBILE PHONES

Within a family context, the mobile phone stands out quite clearly as the seminal ICT. But what makes the mobile phone unique? I suggest that mobile phones are unique for two reasons, and I will discuss each reason in turn.

First, mobile phones, started not as devices to enter into the digital environment but instead as portable telephones, were normalized as a means to maintain ties with significant others. Although Twitter and other mobile applications are changing how mobile phones are understood, the primary purpose of mobile phones is still to communicate with significant others. Indeed, many people decide to keep a landline phone for business communication, and their mobile phone for personal communication. They specialize their mobile phone activity even further by e-mailing friends they are less familiar with, texting people they are a little more familiar with, and then finally calling those people whom they would consider significant others. People across the globe are adept at using the mobile phone for this purpose. James E. Katz and Mark Aakhus (2002) label this phenomenon "perpetual contact", and it describes perfectly the broad range of research that explores the ways that people maintain constant contact with their significant others using mobile phones. Ling et al. (2012), analyzing the texting patterns of mobile phone users, show that most people text to around five or fewer people. But we don't need research to know that when we call and text someone, it's generally people with whom we share strong emotional bonds, and that by default will be family members.

Second, the mobile phone is unique because it provides contextual freedom. Kakihara and Sorensen (2002) argue that human interaction occurs in three dimensions—spatial, temporal, and contextual, and the mobile phone increases flexibility for the user along all three. It goes without saying that being in the DE allows you to communicate with anyone, anywhere as long as they also have access to the DE. You can communicate asynchronously via e-mail—an e-mail can be sent, and the receiver can open and respond when there is time in her daily routine to do so. The mobile phone, however, adds the new dimension of context. Because of its portability and size, it allows the user to enter the DE wherever she happens to be in the PE. While in a meeting at work, while riding on the bus, while waiting in the checkout line, even while enduring an uneventful dinner with a blind date you wished you hadn't gone on, you can enter the DE through your mobile phone.

Imagine attending a funeral. This is a rather somber event. Using an electronic device during such an occasion where solemnity is the norm would incur stares and scowls. Hauling out a laptop or tablet, although they have gotten smaller over the years, is just not possible. Also, the laptop and tablet are understood in social life as unassociated with important communication. However, the mobile phone is small enough that the aura of seriousness can be maintained, and the device is understood to be a mechanism through which necessary communication takes place. The person who uses his mobile phone—granted in hush tones, and briefly—could be tolerated. The different contexts that we navigate in the physical environment are less of a barrier to entry into the digital environment if one has access to a mobile phone.[2] It is the contextual freedom the mobile phone affords that truly makes this technology unique and allows people to be networked individuals.

THE AFRICAN AMERICAN FAMILY

There are several structural realities present in the African American family. First, African Americans living in what is understood to be the traditional nuclear family are a minority (Cherlin 2006). Research published in 2010 shows that the share of unmarried births to single mothers within each racial group was: whites—17%, Hispanics—50%, and for African Americans—70% (Hummer and Hamilton 2010). Further, the 2010 Census shows that the percentage of African Americans living in husband and wife households was 28%. The percentages for whites, Hispanics, and Asians were 51%, 50%, and 60%, respectively (Census.Gov 2010b). Second, African Americans tend to have large extended families, with blood related kin and family friends brought into the family structure (McAdoo 1998, Taylor et al. 1997). By extended family, I mean blood relatives (cousins, aunts, uncles, grandparents) as well as persons not related by blood (family friends) but who are understood to be a part of one's immediate family. Third, African American families tend to have at least two geographic centers. Almost every African American family in the North has a close blood relative or two "down south". Conversely, almost every African American family has a close blood relative "up north". In my case, two of my uncles left during the 1960s and moved to Richmond, Virginia and Brooklyn, New York, respectively, where they started very large families. This bifurcated nature of African American extended kin networks is due to what scholars call the "Great Migration". The Great Migration is a term used to describe the mass exodus of African Americans from the southern United States to northern and western industrial centers like Chicago, Detroit, and New York City from approximately 1910 to 1970 (see Tolnay 2003 for discussion of the sociological research on this phenomenon). By the time the migration was over, the percentage of African Americans living in the American South dropped from 90% to 50% (Tolnay 1997).

These structural realities produce a great deal of familial complexity. It is not enough to be aware of one's immediate family and both sets of grandparents, nor to be only cognizant of people in your hometown. Ties need to be maintained with a wide array of people spread out across the country. But African Americans have managed to maintain connections with disparate family members. Although recent research on extended kin networks—their causes, consequences, and maintenance—is thin (Johnson 2004), what is available suggests that the ties binding black families together are quite strong (Stack 1974; Roy and Burton 2007), with surveys showing that 90% of African Americans consider themselves close to their families (Hatchett & Jackson 1993). African Americans had been able to maintain some degree of "perpetual contact" in the physical environment before the advent of the mobile phone. Thus, it is worth exploring the cultural patterns associated with these structural realities.

The non-traditional family does not necessarily imply a "broken" home, as might be suspected from media stereotypes. The fact that African American men do not live with their children does not necessarily mean that they are non-existent from the lives of their children. African American men who are not a part of the nuclear family are more likely to provide practical assistance and emotional support than white men who are similarly positioned. The assistance may not be economic—a fact attributable to lower socioeconomic status—but instead is mainly about communication and parenting (Sarkisian 2007). This tendency to help, albeit in non-economic ways, is not restricted to only fathers. In Chapter 4, I discussed this same tendency to provide support vis-à-vis extended family members and friends (recall the discussion on "helping ideology").

I can recall from my own experience finding out that someone I thought was a "cousin" had no relation to me at all. For all practical purposes, she was as related to me as any other cousin who I saw during the holidays and summer months. It wasn't until my twenties that I found out she was taken in by my grandmother when she was very young and raised like a member of the family. This is an example of the "helping ideology", and goes a long way towards bonding non-traditional families and extended families.

There are other cultural properties of African American families. There are the annual family reunions where extended kin meet to reestablish and strengthen bonds. There are the summer trips of children to an aunt's or uncle's house for an extended stay. Or, the weeklong holiday pilgrimages where entire families travel to stay in a brother's or sister's house. In my experiences the flow of travel is often from north to south, with families that have left return to pay their respects to the kin they've left.

Tyler Perry's *Madea* series of movies illustrates the interconnectedness of African American families. Perry's families are always such that family friends, grandparents, aunts, uncles, and cousins all participate in family accomplishments.

His most popular character, the grandmother Madea, is constantly meddling in her children and grandchildren's affairs. Perry's movies, in part, are so popular because they connect with the everyday realities of African American family life. His characters face an assortment of challenges familiar to African Americans—unemployment, drug addiction, and divorce among others. Yet, they find ways to overcome these problems through the collective efforts of their immediate and extended family, led by Madea.

All this is to say that African Americans face a structural reality of complex familial networks, and a cultural precedent towards finding ways to maintain familial ties. As Barry Wellman and Lee Rainie show, families of all ethnoracial groups have responded to the individualizing effects of society by becoming "networked individuals". I suggest that African Americans follow this trend as well. However, the complexities of African American familial networks provide an even stronger push towards adopting and using mobile phones.

RESEARCH QUESTION

I began this chapter with an excerpt of a report from the Pew Internet and American Life project. This report, published in 2010, stated that minorities are more mobile than whites. They are more likely to own a mobile phone, and more varied in their usage of the mobile phone. I suggested that the Pew findings can be explained by focusing on family differences. The general trend for individuals in Western society has been towards "networked individualism", where they maintain fluid social networks not bound by geography. The complex family structures of African Americans and the willingness to maintain them intensifies these phenomena. The uniqueness of the African American family structure and the practices that have developed around it is a cultural precedent from the physical environment that allowed for the quick adoption and intense use of mobile phones.

One way to approach these issues is to understand how much of African Americans being more mobile is due to the structural realities of familial networks. The first step would be to establish, through regression modeling, the effect of being African American on measures of mobile phone adoption and usage controlling for other socioeconomic factors. The next step would be to include measures of family structure into the model. If family structure variables reduce or eliminate the effect of being African American, then we can say that much of the difference between African Americans and whites is due to structural differences. Thus the research question ordering this study is: *What effect does family structure have on mobile phone adoption?*

DATA

Survey

The data from the "Mobile Access 2010" survey was collected from April 29, 2010, to May 30, 2010. The survey asks respondents questions about the type of technology they own, and their attitudes towards these technologies. The total number of respondents for the sample was 2252. Weights supplied by the Pew Research Center were used for all analyses.

Independent Variables

Controlling variables. Several demographic variables will be included in the analysis. They are not the focus of the analysis and are included in order to hold constant some of the factors that are known to effect technology usage. For example, scholars are well aware that income has a (generally positive) effect on if and how a person uses technology. Thus, I include variables like income here to control for them, and hold them constant. I can then make claims such as "with income and education the same for any given respondent, the effect of race is—". The variables included as controls are age, education, gender, employment, and family income and are shown in Table 5.1.

Ethnoracial Group and Family Structure Variables. The independent variables of interest—the variables assumed to be causing the differences in mobile phone usage—are ethnoracial group and family structure. Ethnoracial group is straightforward, measured by white, African American, Hispanic, and an "other" category that combines respondents who are not one of the three largest ethnoracial groups into one category.

Family structure is measured in three ways—marital status, number of dependents (children under the age of 18) and number of extended kin (number of adults reported living in the household). With respect to marital status, respondents have been placed into four categories: married, living with partner, divorced-separated-widowed, and never married-single. The decision to create these particular marital status categories was born first out of practicality, and second by classifying based on commonality. Practically, the data set is too small to support an analysis of each marital status. Thus, marital statuses were classified based on commonality. Marriage, a family structure backed by the state and considered the norm for society, will be one category. People who are divorced, separated, and widowed share the fact that they were once married. These statuses are combined into a second category. People who are living with partners (cohabitating) are similar to married couples. However, research shows that both in objective outcomes (Cohan and Kleinbaum 2002) and subjective perceptions (Nock 1995), cohabitation is distinct from marriage. Thus living with partner is a third category. Finally, people who have never been married and people who are single are combined into a fourth category. The univariate statistics for family structure variables are shown in Table 1.

Table 5.1. Univariate Statistics for Independent Variables N = 2252

Variable	Freq (%)	Variable	Freq (%)
Education		Gender	
Less Than High School	12.6	Male	48.4
High School	32.0	Female	51.6
Some College (Including 2-Yr. Coll)	27.0		
Bachelor's Degree and Above	28.4	Race/Ethnicity	
		White	70.6
Family Income		African American	11.9
Less than $10,000	9.0	Hispanic	11.4
Between $10,000 and $30,000	24.5	Other	6.2
Between $30,000 and $75,000	37.8		
More than $75,000	28.7	Marital Status	
		Married	52.0
Employment		Living with partner	7.2
Full Time	44.7	Divorced, Separated, or Widowed	19.2
Part Time	13.0	Never Been Married or Single	21.7
Retired	18.2		
Unemployed	17.8		

Continuous Variables				
	Mean	SD	Min	Max
Age	46.05	18.29	18	97
Number of Extended Kin	.35	.71	0	4
Number of Dependents	.55	1.01	0	7

Dependent Variables

Ownership. The rates of ownership were measured through the question: "*Do you have a cell phone or a Blackberry or iPhone or other device that is also a cell phone?*"

As per the Pew report, 80% of whites reported owning a cell [mobile] phone, while 87% of African Americans and Hispanics report using a mobile phone. Respondents who did not fit into one of the three largest ethnoracial groups were, unfortunately, condensed into one measure labeled "other". This group reported rates similar to whites, at 81%.

Raw Measures of Making Calls and Texting. There were two raw measures of mobile phone frequency measured: calling and texting. They are "raw" in that they say nothing about purpose or duration, only the average number of times they called or texted in a day. For making phone calls the respondent was asked: *How many phone calls do you make and receive on your cell phone?* The range for this variable was 0 (minimum) to 500 (maximum). The mean was 13.10, with a standard deviation of 28.4. For sending text messages, the respondent was asked: *On an average day, about how many text messages do you send and receive on your cell phone?* These measures had to be transformed to make them amenable to regression modeling. You can see these transformations in Appendix A.

Mobile Phone Activities. Eleven questions from the "Mobile 2010" survey asked respondents about what they do with their mobile phone, and the frequency of doing them. Five questions focused on calling, and asked respondents *"How often do you call to…* (1) *Say hello and chat,* (2) *Report where you are or check on where someone is,* (3) *To coordinate where you are physically meeting someone,* (4) *To do things related to work,* (5) *Have a long conversation to discuss important things"?* Six questions focused on texting, and asked respondents *"How often do you send or receive text messages to…* (1) *Say hello and chat,* (2) *Report where you are or check on where someone is,* (3) *Coordinate where you are physically meetings someone,* (4) *Do things related to work,* (5) *Have a long exchange discussing important personal matters,* (6) *Exchange information quietly when you can't make a voice call"?* Respondents could reply "never", "less often than a few times", "a few times a week", "at least once a day", and "several times a day". It is possible to reduce these eleven activities into a fewer number with only a minimal loss of explanatory power using factor analysis (see Appendix B). A factor analysis produces four factors. These factors can be understood to be tapping into a general dimension of mobile phone activity. These general activities are (1) chatting using text messaging, (2) using the phone for work-related activities via text or voice, (3) using the phone for coordination via text or voice, and (4) chat using voice.

In sum, there are seven dependent variables—a measure of ownership, a raw measure of the number of phone calls, a raw measure of text messages, and four measures of mobile phone activities—"text chat", "work", "coordinate", and "voice chat".

METHOD

Stepwise regression modeling is used to address the research question. In stepwise regression modeling, an initial set of variables are included in a model, and its effects on the dependent variables are assessed. More variables are included in subsequent models and the changes in preceding variables are assessed. For each of the seven dependent variables, two models are run. The first model includes control variables and race. The second model retains the initial independent variables, and then includes measures of the family. Ownership is a binary dependent variable, meaning there are only two responses "yes" or "no", and is modeled using binary logistic regression and estimates are presented in odds-ratios[3]. For the remaining dependent variables, standard linear regression is used. The regression models shown are simplified, with only standardized coefficients (betas) shown. For this type of analysis where comparisons of effects are needed an analysis of betas is preferable. When trying to make predictions based upon the model, then unstandardized coefficients, given in the units of the dependent variable, are preferable.

ANALYSIS

Regression Models

Ownership. As expected age, education, income, and employment status are significant, and affect ownership in predictable ways. For example, age is negatively associated with ownership, as an increase in one year of age corresponds to a .034% decrease (1 − .966) in the odds of owning a mobile phone. For education, those respondents with some college or higher are more likely to own a mobile phone. Thus, a person with some college or technical school is 42% more likely (1.42 − 1) and a person with a bachelor's degree is 96% (1.96 − 1) more likely to own a phone than a respondent with a HS diploma (the comparison, or reference group). There are only slight changes in direction or magnitude.

The effect of being African American is to increase the likelihood of owning a mobile phone. They are 89% more likely than other racial groups to own a mobile phone, and this is taking into account controls. The main focus of Table 5.2 is on the change in the effect from Model 1 to Model 2 once family variables are included. There is no change in direction and a slight increase in magnitude. The purpose of showing this table is to give a sense of how all the remaining variables are done. An initial model presents the controls plus African American. Then, a second model introduces family variables.

Table 5.2. Binary Logistic Regression Model Showing Log Odds for Owning a Mobile Phone

Variables	Mobile Phone Ownership	
	Model 1	Model 2
Controls		
Age	.966***	.967***
Female	1.13*	1.14*
Education (Comparison Variable is HS Diploma)		
– Less than HS	.990	1.03
– Some College/Tech School	1.42***	1.43***
– Bachelor's Degree or More	1.96***	1.92***
Family Income (Compared to Income Between $30 and $75,000		
– Less than $10,000	.457***	.470***
– Between $10 and $30000	.552***	.563***
– More than $75,000	1.99***	1.96***
Employment (Compared to Employed Full Time)		
– Part Time	.572***	.576***
– Retired	.477***	.477***
– Unemployed	.550***	.559***
Race (African Americans compared to all other ethnoracial groups)		
– African American	1.89***	1.93***
Family Type		
Marital Status (Comparison Variable is Married)		
– Cohabitating		1.14
– Divorced/Separated/Widowed		.813*
– Never Married or Single		.992
Family Size		
– Number of Children in Home		1.01
– Number of Adults in Home		.874**
Nagelkerke R^2	.233	.236

Raw Mobile Phone Frequency and Mobile Phone Activities. Recall that there are two measures of mobile phone frequency—calling and text, and there are four dimensions of mobile phone activity—"text chat", "work", "coordinate", and "voice chat". The regression models for each independent variable are presented in Appendices D and E. Readers may wish to explore these models. However, a direct way of comparing the effects (parameter estimates) of being African American before and after the inclusion of family variables is to place these effects in one table (Figure 5.1). Dependent variables are organized to maximize clarity and to make it easier to compare and contrast effects. The coordinating factor is not included, as being African American is not statistically significant.

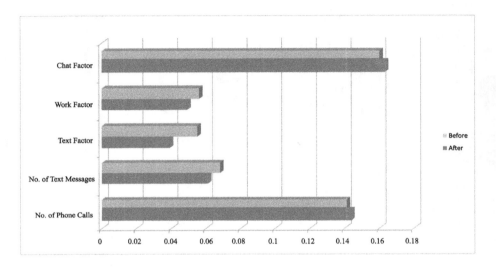

Figure 5.1. The Effects of Being African American before and after the Inclusion of Family Variables.

We can draw general conclusions about the relationship between mobile phone usage, African Americans, and family variables using Figure 5.1. First, for measures that are composed of texting or contain some element of texting, the effect of race is decreased (but not eliminated) with the inclusion of family variables. Thus, the effect of being African American on the raw number of text messages sent and received as well as "text chat" and "work" decreases after the inclusion of family variables. This finding suggests that with respect to texting, African Americans take on the property of "networked individuals".

But the mobile phone is not only about texting. Second, for measures that are entirely about calling, the effect of race does not decrease with the inclusion of family variables. Instead, there is a slight *increase*. Accordingly, the effect of being African American on "voice chat" and raw number of phone calls increases with the inclusion of family variables.

Third, the overall effect of being African American is stronger with regards to voice than text. The difference is quite large, with the effect for text measures being around 0.07 or less, and the effect for voice measures being around 0.14 or above. Also, the only variable in which African American has no effect—the factor coordinating—is composed of measures of texting. These last two findings suggest that there is something unique about the African American mobile phone experience. Their interactions in the digital environment, via mobile phones, are characterized by a much higher degree of voice than other ethnoracial groups.

CONCLUSION

I began this chapter by citing a 2010 report from the Pew Internet and American Life project showing that minorities are more mobile than whites. They adopt mobile phones at higher rates and are more varied in their usage of mobile phones. I decided to look at this phenomenon through a digital practice perspective. I focused on the structure and culture of the African American family, and suggested that this is one reason why African Americans are more mobile than whites. In my reasoning, the digital environment simply provided new leverage for old behaviors. The structural realities of complex families, and the cultural practices associated with maintaining them are simply imported into the digital environment via mobile phones.

In teasing out the effects of being African American and various family variables, a bit of nuance has been added to this idea. There is a difference between texting and voice. For dependent variables that measure texting, the effect of being African American is minimal, and is reduced even further when family variables are included. When voice calling is the measure, the effect of being African American is substantially higher. Further, the inclusion of these family variables produces a slight increase in this effect. Thus, the digital practice identified in this research is the use of voice—not necessarily text—to maintain family ties.

This goes against the general assumption that it is the constant texting that characterizes mobile phone use. We think of the young and the tech savvy using their mobile phones in classrooms, on buses, in long lines, at dinner tables. For African Americans, voice calling is prominent. Even controlling for age, income, education and other variables, African Americans still use their mobile phones for voice more than other ethnoracial groups. This is, I suggest, due to the fact the voice is a better means through which emotional support can be provided. One can organize logistics, check-in with significant others, or just say hi using text. However, the limited amount of characters per text and the lack of social cues hamstring texting when one wishes to communicate deep meaning or convey feelings. African Americans can, regardless of where they are in the physical environment, use the mobile phone as an on-ramp into the digital environment. They then use the digital environment as new leverage for old behaviors, continuing maintaining and strengthening family ties.

CHAPTER SIX

The Digital Practice of Maintaining Digital Enclaves

INTRODUCTION

There are a multitude of websites that cater to African Americans. Some websites have as their explicit purpose the selling of entertainment products to a user base. The website for Black Entertainment Television, BET.com, is an example of this. Other websites may focus on disseminating information, such as Electronic Urban Entertainment Web. Still others take on an expressly political purpose, such as the website for the NAACP (www.naacp.org). Despite these differences, each website contributes in its own way to producing rhetoric unique to African Americans. They offer a space for African Americans to develop ideas, explanations, and narratives that contest mainstream interpretations of societal events. In this chapter I will discuss the historical antecedents in the physical environment that underpin this digital practice and discuss results from a case study of a website I consider an exemplar of this practice, the online magazine *The Root*.

APPLYING A DIGITAL PRACTICE PERSPECTIVE

As in Chapter 5, I use a digital practice perspective to order my thinking, and try to answer three basic questions. I provide brief answers here, and then spend the bulk of the chapter developing them further:

1. *What historical and current structural conditions are important?* Historically, African Americans have constructed separate spaces for discussion of uniquely black issues and concerns. This began as black only spaces hidden from whites during the Slavery era, and has continued in many forms to the present day, such as juke joints and barbershops. Presently, African Americans endure micro aggressions in white dominated spaces and a level of "othering" not witnessed by other groups. The use of minority spaces of dialogue—what will be discussed as counterpublics in more detail below—can be a means to counteract this condition. These counterpublics allow African Americans to learn more about uniquely black viewpoints, and to air their sentiments without fear of recriminations.

2. *How do the properties of the digital environment create the conditions for new practices?* Because of the decreased cost of manipulating symbolic information, there is expansion of potential counterpublics online. The decreased cost has an effect on both producers and consumers. On the production end, anyone can make their ideas available, through text, audio, video, or a combination of both. On the consumption end, it is easy for people to participate in sites that have been constructed. In Chapter 3 I talked about the various types of groups that can form more easily in the digital environment (see Table 3.2). Sharing and cooperating are the easiest types of group activities and most counterpublics will most likely exhibit these behaviors above all others. Users will share by posting their comments or submitting pictures and articles. They will also cooperate by making a commitment (a small one) to replying to others' comments.

3. *Within which layer(s) is this leveraging occurring?* I suggest that the human, content, and web layers may all be equal locations for leveraging. Given this, there are at least three possible approaches to this study, with each approach emphasizing a different layer. One approach, emphasizing the human layer, could be to simply conduct a survey of users of a website understood to be a digital hush harbor, asking questions about why they use the website and the type of questions engendered. Because I explored the human layer in other chapters, I'd like to focus

on different layers for this case study. The layers I will focus on for this case study are the web layer and the content layer. In the web layer HTML (hypertext markup language) allows webpages to interlink and form a blogosphere or echo chamber. The idea is that links from one website to another suggest homophily between the two sites, and act as an explicit endorsement of the content of that site. Meanwhile, the content layer houses the information produced and consumed on webpages—the articles on *The Root* and the replies to those articles by users. Studying this layer could provide insight into the types of narratives and frames constructed on *The Root*.

PUBLICS AND COUNTERPUBLICS

In *The Structural Transformation of the Public Sphere: An Inquiry into a Category of Bourgeois Society*, Jürgen Habermas (1989 [1962]) introduces the notion of a public sphere, and narrates its decline. The public sphere, according to Habermas, initially developed in European countries in the 18th century as a mediator between private concerns (family life, business, and labor), and spheres in which the state had authority (police, law, government). The public sphere at that time was composed of a set of institutions through which private citizens could come together. Habermas gives as examples the coffeehouses of London, the salons of Paris, and the literary houses of Germany. Those who met may have been from different milieus, but they were united in their exclusion from state power. Habermas (1989) writes:

> "Transcending the barriers of social hierarchy, the bourgeois met here with the socially prestigious but politically uninfluential nobles as 'common' human beings. The decisive element was not so much the political equality of the members but their exclusiveness in relation to the political realm of absolutism as such: social equality was possible at first only as an equality outside the state" (34–35).

Although the people who populated these coffeehouses and salons could be both commoner and nobleman, they were generally property owners. Because of this, Habermas called this space for meeting the *bourgeois* public sphere. It was here in the bourgeois public sphere that public opinion was produced. Individual interests were subordinated to the development of a common goal through rational debate. Issues were defined and problematized, and solutions were articulated.

However, this bourgeois public sphere as it was initially formulated in the 1700s changed form with the growth of industry, mass consumption, and mass media. In modern society, Habermas argues, the bourgeois public sphere had disintegrated. As the size of governments increased, they became more involved in private matters, especially the workings of business. At the same time business and corporations grew in size and influence, and became more involved in the political process. Through mass media outlets, political and economic elites could control public opinion. Rational debate leading to a consensus had given way to groups organized by elites competing for their own self-interest. The bourgeois public sphere as it had been originally formulated was lost. Habermas saw this as the decline of a healthy deliberative democracy.

Some scholars take umbrage with the notion that a public sphere as understood by Habermas is conducive to a healthy democracy. They argue that separate spheres populated by racial minorities, women, and homosexuals are necessary in order for the views of these groups to germinate and solidify into coherent narratives. The work of Nancy Fraser (1990) and Michael Dawson (1995, 2001) have been influential in this regard. Both Fraser and Dawson argue that the social inequalities present in society are rearticulated in the public sphere, such that it is difficult for weaker groups in society to get their opinions heard. The bourgeois public sphere is not inclusive and is primarily a space for white, middle class men to debate the issues of the day. And so any group consensus emerging from the bourgeois public is only ever the opinions of this group, and the interests of this group did not necessarily reflect the interest of other groups. Thus separate spheres, what Fraser termed "subaltern counterpublics", are needed to support the deliberations of women and minorities. These subaltern counterpublics can be physical spaces for debate, but also literary journals, radio, and television outlets.

Fraser argues primarily from a feminist perspective, while Dawson develops his argument with a focus on African Americans. For this reason, much of my analysis is ordered by Dawson's writings. Dawson agrees with Fraser that gender and class exclude certain groups from participating in the *bourgeois* public sphere. Dawson goes further, and argues that the institutionalization of discrimination in American society not only excludes African Americans from formal institutions of deliberative democracy, but also from many of the subaltern counterpublics that Fraser points to. Thus, from the late 1800s until the 1960s a "Black counterpublic" existed that allowed African Americans to critique both the formal and informal levers of government. Dawson (1995) writes: "An independent Black press, the production and circulation of socially and politically sharp popular Black music and the Black church have provided the institutional bases for the Black counterpublic since the Civil War" (210).

But, Dawson argues that the heyday of the black counterpublic is over:

"A Black public sphere does not exist in contemporary America, if by that we mean a set of institutions, communication networks and practices which facilitate debate of causes and remedies to the current combination of political setbacks and economic devastation facing major segments of the Black community, and which facilitate the creation of oppositional formations and sites.... More precisely, what no longer exists is a black counterpublic of the type described by Fraser" (p. 201).

Given the vibrant dialogue amongst African Americans on radio, in barbershops and churches, and in the digital environment I disagree with Dawson's statement. It is possible that Dawson's conclusions would be different had he formulated them in the present day of distributed networks, social networking sites, and Twitter. The proliferation of ICTs and the migration of public dialogue to the digital environment mean we need new ways of describing public and counterpublics. This is where I turn next.

THE NETWORKED PUBLIC SPHERE VERSUS SEGMENTATION AND POLARIZATION

There are at least two ways to think about deliberative democracy in the digital environment (DE). One way is to assume that the emergence of the DE has led to a democratization of communication, cultural production, and political participation. This view is exemplified by Yochai Benkler's notion of a networked public sphere (2006). In the DE, Benkler begins, the connections are multidimensional. There are numerous clusters of websites that can provide information to the user, and a user can receive information from any of them. Because there are so many routes to acquiring information it is easier for everyday citizens to be listeners and speakers of public dialogue, and it is more difficult for governments to control what is being heard and what is being said. Benkler argues that although the web is not the completely flat utopia it was once thought to be it is a marked improvement over the hierarchical mass media of the physical environment. The web is slightly hierarchical, with clusters of moderately read sites interconnected with a few dominant sites. Benkler's networked public sphere, a vision of society where debate is carried out in a public forum, is in essence a digitized form of the Habermasian public sphere.

Another view of the DE vis-à-vis democracy is more disparaging. Because information is easy to manipulate in the DE, there is an exponential growth in what is produced. All that information sounds like a good thing, but some scholars see this as decreasing dialogue and thus hampering the democratic process. People are free to be both listeners and speakers, but they will only listen to and speak to those who are like themselves. One notable proponent of this view is Cass Sunstein. Sunstein argues that the Internet produces two distinct, yet related processes of segmentation and polarization (2001). Segmentation refers to groups of users producing and consuming content in distinct worlds, although they are in theoretically the same environment. These groups then become polarized, as they lose the nuance of opposing viewpoints. Another iteration of this argument is Eli Pariser's *Filter Bubble* (2011). Pariser writes that the customization of search engines and web portals like Google and Yahoo hide information from users. A user's search history determines what appears on home pages and in search engines, meaning that different users will get different versions of what is new, noteworthy, and important.

Table 6.1 summarizes the types of dialogues for the physical and digital environment. In the physical environment I see the nurturing and maintenance of a counterpublic for ethnoracial minorities, women, and groups with different lifestyles as essential to a healthy democracy. My opinions are the same for the digital environment. Benkler is correct when he writes that the networked public sphere in the digital environment is preferable to the monopolized media production in the physical environment. But from an African American perspective, I wouldn't mind a bit of segmentation and polarization. My point of departure will be research done by Matthew Hindman (2009), presented in his book *The Myth of Digital Democracy*. Hindman, using network analysis, shows rather convincingly that for any topic network traffic is dominated by only a handful of websites. Furthermore, who are the owners of those sites? You guessed it. White males. Usually with degrees from prestigious universities.

And so, while there are more nodes of dialogue in the DE, *the ideological content may not deviate that much from the handful of news outlets that dominate the PE*. Dialogue in the DE is still dominated by a select stratum of society. For this reason, it will benefit African Americans and other minority groups, as well as groups in the working class or in alternative lifestyles, to be segmented away. Instead of entering into a dialogue on these major sites, where one's issues may not be raised or when raised not given appropriate consideration, it will be more advantageous to find an alternative space where only others like you can communicate and nurture an opinion.

Table 6.1. Comparisons of Dialogue in the Physical Environment and the Digital Environment

Physical Environment	
Public Sphere	Counterpublics
Jürgen Habermas (1962)	Nancy Fraser (1990), Michael Dawson (1995, 2001)
Bourgeois = Property Owners, Middle Class	Subordinated Groups
Liberalism	Group Concerns
Hegemonic	Counterhegemonic
Digital Environment	
Networked Public Sphere	Segmentation and Polarization
Yochai Benkler (2006)	Cass Sunstein (2007)
Information from Nonmarket Actors	"The Daily Me" produced by dominant Internet entities
Clusters of nested, moderately read sites	Echo Chambers
Viable Option to Concentrated Mass Media	Strong understanding of group concerns

AFRICAN AMERICAN COUNTERPUBLICS ONLINE

For African Americans, the need for a viable counterpublic in both the PE and DE may be more acute than for other groups. There are at least two reasons for this. First, there is a historical reason. The public statements made by African Americans critiquing the unfairness of the American social structure were often met with a level of physical violence or social sanctioning rarely experienced by other groups. African Americans have had to develop what James Scott (1990) has termed a "hidden transcript", or discourse that takes places outside of the purview of those in power. In the Antebellum South the repercussions of discussing these issues were, among other things, physical beatings. Scholars have written of slaves forming secret "hush harbors" to produce uniquely black rhetoric outside of the gaze of their masters. Byrne (2008) provides this explanation of hush harbors: "the places where slaves gathered to participate in various aspects of public life, hidden, unnoticed, and especially inaudible to their white masters" (17). These hush harbors, albeit in different forms, continued to be a significant component of African American life after slavery. Here is Vorris Nunley describing hush harbors, placing both the spaces produced before and after the end of slavery into one theoretical construct:

"In these hush harbor spaces, Black rhetors and speakers were free to engage in and deploy otherwise heavily monitored practices, knowledges, and rhetorics disallowed in the public sphere under the disciplining gaze of Whites and Whiteness. In informal, unofficial meeting places such as cane breaks, woods, praise houses, funeral parlors, jook joints, the Chitlin' Circuit, and their contemporary manifestations in beauty shops and barbershops, hush harbor geographies were/are quasi-public hidden spaces where Blackness on parallel, alternative, and lower frequencies circulates. In these spaces, enslaved Africans and African Americans can come in from the wilderness of the racially mediated public sphere" (Nunley 2011: 23–24).

In post-Civil Rights America African Americans no longer face the threat of physical violence. However, the policing of black discussions are now done with more subtlety, in predominantly white spaces where minorities must conform to white practices in order to fit in.

Consider this imaginary example, likely repeated in many work environments. The African American employee, in company meetings, finds herself subtly rejected because of her blackness. Co-workers are uneasy talking to her and find others to chat with during meetings. Her opinions are delegitimized, not seen as universal but from the perspective of her group. In casual conversation it is hinted at that she is an affirmative action hire, and so on. In such a case, where she is one or the only African American person and she has an eye on career advancement, it is in her best interest to endure these slights and do her best to "fit in". These slights are labeled "microaggressions" by psychologists (see Sue 2010). These microaggressions are an everyday reality in the lives of minorities.[1]

In such a situation, she may find it necessary to retire to a safe space to vent. As Scott (1990) writes:

"It is as if the 'voice'…they are refused in the public transcript finds its full-throated expression backstage. The frustration, tension, and control necessary in public give way to a unbridled retaliation in a safer setting, where the accounts of reciprocity are, symbolically at least, finally balanced" (p. 38).

In the DE, this retaliation can take the form of instant messaging other African Americans, tweeting something with the hash tag #racism, or describing her experiences on websites.

There is a second reason why the need for a counterpublic is more acute for African Americans. African Americans have been constructed as the undesirable "other" in American society to a degree unequaled by other groups. This understanding undergirds research into anti-blackness (Sexton 2008) and the black-white status continuum (Feagin 2001). The underlying assumption is that throughout American history whites have defined their racial identity and the privileges associated with it through a rejection of blackness. Other groups who enter into American society must then find their place between these two poles, gaining "intermediate status" as they approximate whiteness (Feagin 2000). Within this context, having a place where counterhegemonic ideas and frames are produced where you are not, in the words of W.E.B Dubois (1903), "a problem"[2], is indispensable: if not for the practical reasons of advancing political gains, then at least for the psychological benefit of constructing ideas that do not paint blackness and African Americans as a congenital malady in American society.

The idea that I put forth here, that African Americans have developed their own spaces for dialogue in the digital environment, has been the topic of several pieces of research. Anna Everett (2009) examined the content of several African American newspapers that have begun publishing online. What Everett shows is that the transfer to the digital environment has changed little in terms of the content and mission: "This survey of select historic black presses' migration to the Internet clearly reveals their commitment to continue the struggle for black political, social, cultural, and economic survival and prosperity well into the digital age" (2009: 105–106). Later, she writes that these newspapers in the DE "disseminate...black counterhegemonic interpretations of local and global events" (2009: 106). Byrne (2007) explored the discussion boards of the social networking site *BlackPlanet* (www.blackplanet.com). Byrne's major concern was the ability of online discussion forums to catalyze social movements. Towards this end, she found little evidence that the users of *BlackPlanet* catalyzed their discussions into meaningful action. However, of interest to this chapter are the discussions themselves. Byrne found that the users were heavily invested in topics related to the community, and issues regarding race and race relations were the most popular (2007). Thus, although these discussions may not have led to action according to Byrne's analysis, clearly they constituted what Fraser and other scholars would call a counterpublic. *BlackPlanet* provided a space for African American users to explore issues relating to them that are often overlooked in mainstream spaces. Everett's and Byrne's work addresses the black counterpublic broadly conceived. Moreover, research shows that blacks form their own separate communities around more specific issues. Thus Kvasny and Igwe (2008) show that black Internet users developed their own race-specific discourse surrounding HIV/AIDS, and Mehra et al. (2004) illustrate a community website for African American women to discuss issues pertaining to them.

THE ROOT AS AN EXAMPLE OF A DIGITAL ENCLAVE

For past chapters, I used the digital practice perspective to generate hypotheses or generate conclusions. For this chapter, the perspective provides a context through which I will explore an example of a black counterpublic. It may not be appropriate to use the term counterpublic, given the porousness of a website in the digital environment—it's not like the barbershops of today or juke joints of the past where the presence of a white person would be rare. I can recall from my own experiences growing up that I never saw a white person in a black-owned barbershop or bar. Furthermore, interaction online can be anonymous, removing racial coding from the equation. Instead, I'd like to use the term digital enclave. Enclave connotes a neighborhood that is understood to be for, and mainly populated by, a single ethnicity. And so a digital enclave is a website that is understood to be for, and is mainly populated by, a single ethnoracial group.

The online magazine *The Root* (www.theroot.com) may be understood as a digital enclave. *The Root*, owned by the *Washington Post*, was launched to be a "Slate for black readers", according to one of its founders, Harvard University professor Henry Louis Gates Jr. (Ahrens 2008). It is a popular site, with an Alexa rank of 4,268.[3]

This case study will be done in two ways, roughly corresponding to the two layers I have chosen to focus on. First, I will explore the network environment that *The Root* is embedded in. By analyzing the connections between *The Root* and other websites, we can judge the degree to which *The Root* occupies a separate space in the digital environment. Simply put, if *The Root* is tightly connected with websites that are not used primarily by African Americans to discuss issues pertaining to the African American experience, *The Root* cannot be considered in any real sense a digital enclave. Also, we can explore the degree to which *The Root* is connected to other African American websites. There is in all likelihood a convergence of separate black spaces. *The Root* can be seen as its own ethnic enclave or as a component of a wider ethnic enclave composed of numerous African American-themed websites. Second, a content analysis is done on a small subset of articles and discussion board posts. The content analysis will focus on the political discourse, and explore some of the themes of this discourse.

NETWORK ENVIRONMENT OF THE ROOT

Exploring the network environment of *The Root* will be done by analyzing the URL (uniform resource locator) citations on *The Root* and a sample of popular websites. A URL citation is the writing of a web address—such as www.espn.

com or www.yahoo.com on a webpage. In this way one website references, or cites, another. The URL citation can also be a hyperlink, but it does not have to be. Both the owners of websites and the users of websites—the former through the writing of HTML or changing the pages on the site and the latter by putting names of websites into discussion boards—supply citations to other pages.

These citations can be interpreted as endorsements for the contents of that site and also are a practical means for the web surfer to find relevant content. Collecting the citations between *The Root* and other relevant websites and presenting this information in a network diagram can reveal the environment in which *The Root* is situated. The network diagram is a visual representation of the interlinking between websites, with circles representing websites, and arrows representing the URL citations between them. Websites that contain citations to each other suggest homophily amongst those sites.

The sample consists of 41 websites (see Table 6.1). This sample is one of convenience, based upon the top websites for their given genre as listed by Alexa.com. Nearly half of the sites, 20, were the top African American sites measured by web traffic as listed by Alexa.com; 10 were the top news sites; and 10 were the top opinion sites, again based upon web traffic measures by Alexa.com. This is a relatively small number of websites given the vastness of the web. However, research suggests that web traffic follows a power law distribution, and that most web traffic is concentrated within a small set of websites (Hindman 2009). This holds both across the web in general, such that Facebook and Google dominate web traffic, but also within genres, such that a website like *Huffington Post* dominates the liberal news reading audience. Thus, for a case study like the present one, a relatively small number of websites can produce valid conclusions.[4] URL citations are collected and analyzed using the software Webometric Analyst (http://lexiurl.wlv.ac.uk/index.html).

The raw data consists of a total of 87,629 URL citations. Select raw data used in the construction of the network diagram is presented in Table 6.2. The websites are shown, the number of URL Citations (inlinks and outlinks), and the community within which each website belongs (to be discussed below).

The primary purpose of presenting the raw numbers is to give a sense of the popularity of each website and how well connected each site is. The total number of links can be seen together as a measure of importance vis-à-vis other websites in the sample. Further, links can be divided into two types: inlinks and outlinks. Inlinks can be interpreted as votes for a website and a measure of visibility or popularity. Consider for example, a URL citation on *Huffington Post* for *Fox News*. This would be counted as an inlink for *Fox News*. This inlink suggests that someone within the community of users at *Huffington Post* finds the information on *Fox News* relevant enough for others in her community to read. In this way, websites with more votes can be understood as more popular and central to the network (Freeman 1979). Outlinks, on the other hand, are suggestive of connectivity. Websites with more outlinks to other websites are more connected within the network. Theoretically, users who are visiting a more connected website have access to a wider variety of other websites and other channels of information. Consider, for example, someone who is interested in pottery that happens to visit a connected website that has several URL citations to other websites on pottery. This user has at her disposal potentially more channels of information than the user who visits a less connected website about the same topic.

With this understanding of links, a few points can be made about the raw data. First, the websites that one expects to be most connected and most popular— *Yahoo News* (www.news.yahoo.com), *The Huffington Post* (www.huffingtonpost. com), *Google News* (www.news.google.com), *Fox News* (www.foxnews.com), *The New York Times* (www.nytimes.com), and *CNN* (www.cnn.com)—are indeed so. The disparity between these sites and others can be quite large, supporting Hindman's (2009) assertion that the Internet is a highly unequal space. For example, the *Yahoo News* website has a total of 22491 links, whereas *The Network Journal* (www.tnj.com) has a total of 82 total links. *The Root* is, relatively speaking, a mildly popular and somewhat connected site with a total of 1680 total links.

Table 6.2. Raw Data for *The Root* Network Analysis

Name	Alexa Genre Listing	Total Links	Inlinks	Outlinks	Community
theroot.com	None	1680	1012	668	Digital Enclave
eurweb.com	African American	1465	1020	445	Digital Enclave
blackamericaweb. com	African American	956	371	585	Digital Enclave
blackenterprise. com	African American	536	292	244	Digital Enclave
naacp.org	African American	486	476	10	Digital Enclave
s2smagazine.com	African American	338	175	163	Digital Enclave
finalcall.com	African American	262	205	57	Digital Enclave
tadias.com	African American	157	40	117	Digital Enclave
alvinailey.org	African American	139	139	0	Digital Enclave
tnj.com	African American	82	35	47	Digital Enclave
news.yahoo.com	News	22491	5641	16850	Mainstream/AA
huffingtonpost. com	News	18380	6494	11886	Mainstream/AA
news.google.com	News	10713	2081	8632	Mainstream/AA

Table 6.2. *Continued*

Name	Alexa Genre Listing	Total Links	Inlinks	Outlinks	Community
bet.com	African American	2423	1701	722	Mainstream/AA
essence.com	African American	2100	1922	178	Mainstream/AA
blackplanet.com	African American	1057	669	388	Mainstream/AA
vibe.com	African American	738	692	46	Mainstream/AA
okayplayer.com	African American	474	223	251	Mainstream/AA
ebony.com	African American	392	337	55	Mainstream/AA
carolsdaughter.com	African American	310	310	0	Mainstream/AA
thesource.com	African American	119	100	19	Mainstream/AA
cityalert.com	African American	20	18	2	Mainstream/AA
weather.com	News	4032	3848	184	Opinion
nationalreview.com	Opinion	3161	2730	431	Opinion
foxnews.com/politics	Opinion	3002	3002	0	Opinion
tnr.com	Opinion	1741	959	782	Opinion
lucianne.com	Opinion	1470	732	738	Opinion
villagevoice.com	Opinion	1319	1021	298	Opinion
foxnews.com	News	14183	8670	5513	Mainstream
nytimes.com	News	13814	9610	4204	Mainstream
cnn.com	News	11917	8728	3189	Mainstream
reddit.com	News	9460	2747	6713	Mainstream
guardian.co.uk	News	9241	8077	1164	Mainstream
rodonline.type-pad.com	African American	8537	57	8480	Mainstream
pbs.org/wgbh/aia	African American	8092	1162	6930	Mainstream
bbc.co.uk/news	News	7142	3810	3332	Mainstream
theatlantic.com	Opinion	4505	4088	417	Mainstream
townhall.com/columnists	Opinion	3503	938	2565	Mainstream
pbs.org/news-hour	Opinion	2250	2250	0	Mainstream
michellemalkin.com	Opinion	1617	647	970	Mainstream
opposingviews.com	Opinion	954	600	354	Mainstream

Two algorithms are used to produce conclusions from the raw data. Newman's (2006) community algorithm[5] is used to show which websites interlink more than others. The final column in Table 6.2 shows which community each website is in. The four communities that were derived from Newman's community algorithm presented some surprises. The twenty African American websites did not form one community as I had expected. Instead, these sites split into two communities. I have labeled one of these communities "African American Mainstream" primarily because of the high number of links associated with these sites and because widely known and popular sites like *Huffington Post* are members of this community. A second community—made exclusively of African American websites—can be considered an "African American Enclave". *The Root* is a part of this enclave. Along with being homogenous in terms of the type of audience these websites cater to, these websites also possess comparatively fewer links to other communities. This suggests that there is little connection, or a desire for connection, between the digital enclave and other communities. This splitting of African American websites into two communities—one mainstream and one digital enclave—suggests that being by or for African Americans is not enough to determine if a site is a part of a digital enclave as it is discussed in this chapter. In other words, only some African American websites sites tend to interlink exclusively with African American websites. This is quite interesting, but beyond the focus of this chapter to explore. The other two communities that make up this network are not African American in focus. One is composed of mass media outlets, called "News Mainstream", and a second is a collection of less connected, primarily political opinion websites, called simply "News Opinion".

The Fruchterman-Rheingold (1991) algorithm is used to construct the network in Figure 6.1. In order to show the names of websites and then relationships between them more clearly, some nodes have been repositioned. An image of the original network has been superimposed in the bottom left of the figure for reference. Communities defined by the Newman algorithm are color-coded for easy identification. Positions of circles are representative of their centrality in the network—circles that are more towards the center of the diagram have more total inlinks than those towards the periphery. The sizes of the circles represent the number of total links, with large circles having more links (inlink and outlink) than smaller circles.

The network diagram produced can be interpreted as a core-periphery structure. A cluster of websites make up the core of the diagram. These websites are primarily News Mainstream and News Opinion, with a few African American mainstream sites. Around this core of interconnected websites are the websites catering to African Americans. The African American mainstream cluster is closest to the core, with some websites fully a part of the core. However, the websites that make up the African American Enclave cluster, including *The Root,* are fully in the periphery.

In sum, the network analysis confirms the notion that, at least structurally, *The Root* along with other websites aimed at African Americans form a community that can be considered distinct from the more popular websites. From its structural properties, this community can be considered a counterpublic, or in the terms from this chapter, a digital enclave.

Figure 6.1. Network Structure of Top African American and News Websites.

CONTENT ANALYSIS OF POLITICAL COMMENTARY ON *THE ROOT*

This analysis covers one month's worth of content from the politics section of *The Root*[6]. One month of articles, from January 1st, 2013, to January 31st, 2013, were accessed. In total, 25 articles were published during this time span. I also looked at the discussion boards for each article. During this month, some of the more prominent news items were Obama's inauguration speech for his second term in office: gun policy in the wake of the Newtown, Connecticut, shootings; the 40th anniversary of Roe v. Wade; and the birthday of Martin Luther King, Jr. Also, *The Root* ran a special series on education, where civic leaders contributed columns critiquing the state of education in the United States. The findings from this content analysis can be condensed into several themes.

Counterhegemonic Interpretations. Articles on *The Root* focus, as expected, exclusively on the African American perspective. These articles, also as expected, take a decidedly progressive approach to most issues, and highlight the ways in which black people have been discriminated or slighted presently and historically. In short, articles tend to present a counterhegemonic interpretation of social, cultural, and political events—the raison d'être of a counterpublic. A black "spin" was placed on the events of the day, reframing them in ways that fit African American's everyday understanding of them.

For example, the article "GOP's Three-Fifths Compromise"[7] interprets a proposal to change the way electoral votes are allocated as reminiscent of the compromise made between southern and northern states in 1787. That famous proposal decreed that slaves would be considered 3/5 of a person for purposes of representation in the House of Representatives:

> "Instead of electoral votes being awarded to the candidate who wins a popular majority, Republicans intend to assign votes by congressional district—essentially diluting the ballots of African Americans, Hispanics and Asians in metropolitan areas—by giving more leverage to rural counties that are less populated and overwhelmingly white."

As another example, Howard University scholar Ivory Toldson wrote an article entitled "The 'Acting White' Theory Doesn't Add Up".[8] The notion that African American school children, especially males, are anti-intellectual has been used to explain the low test scores for black children. Toldson, after giving empirical evidence that attitudes towards success in school are not linked to actual achievement, writes that:

> "The problem with the Acting White Theory is that it promotes the misconception that black students underachieve because of their corrupted attitudes. Meanwhile, many black students are relegated to under-resourced schools, and they lack motivation because of low expectations from teachers and school leaders, unfair discipline and fewer opportunities for academic enrichment."

Toldson's reinterpretation of why young African Americans do not do as well as other groups in schools converges with my own observations and experiences—as a student and as a high school teacher. In my view, most young African American students are just as eager to learn as other students.

As another example, here is Harvard sociologist Lawrence Bobo giving his perspective on recent data showing that America had become more integrated racially[9]:

"If we artificially set a criterion of 80 percent black neighborhoods as meaning 'segregation,' then yes, we've experienced big declines in racial isolation. The end of segregation? Not hardly. As research by sociologist John Logan showed, a majority of urban blacks still live in neighborhoods that demographers classify as 'highly segregated.' But if you'd read only the headlines, you'd have inferred that we were rapidly becoming 'black no more.'"

Like Toldson's, Bobo's understandings of the reality of the African American experience makes more sense to me than any study purporting the "end of segregation". While living in New York City I saw nothing but segregation. I lived for a time in Jackson Heights, Harlem, and South Bronx. Each of those spaces was dominated by non-whites. Jackson Heights was heavily (middle class mainly) Hispanic, Harlem was heavily black (although this was changing with more white residents) and the South Bronx was overwhelmingly black and Hispanic (there was not a white or Asian resident in the neighborhood where I lived). Even in my small, rural, Southern hometown, the complete opposite of New York City, there was a black area of town and a white area. If one scans a headline from say, CNN, and sees the title "End of Segregation" one may be comforted in knowing that America is moving in a positive direction. However, Bobo paints a more nuanced, and I believe more accurate picture of the US, one of persistent residential segregation.

Emphasizing History. Another theme within *The Root* is its reliance on history and historical context. This manifests itself in two major ways. One way is through the repeated refrains to seminal historical moments such as the Three-Fifths compromise, the Emancipation Proclamation, or the birth or death of a civil rights leader. Another way is by drawing a link between the past trials and tribulations of ancestors and present day racial inequalities.

An example of using historical context comes from an article that commemorates the 150th anniversary of the Emancipation Proclamation. The article uses a letter written by a slave from Maryland to remind readers of the debt owed to ancestors.[10] The letter was written after the proclamation had been signed. However, the slave who had written the letter, Annie Davis, resided in a state still loyal to the Union, and the proclamation did not grant freedom to slaves in those states. The letter was written to Abraham Lincoln asking for her freedom. The author of the column uses excerpts from the letter to highlight the suffering of Davis, and adds:

"Now, 150 years later, as we commemorate the sesquicentennial of the Emancipation Proclamation, I can't help thinking of Annie and all our ancestors. I reflect on how they agitated for their own freedom through protest, revolt, escape, prayer and petition. I am reminded that this observance is about not only the stroke of Lincoln's pen but also the vision of Harriet Tubman, the appeal of abolitionist David Walker and the genius of Frederick Douglass … I'll be grateful to Annie and all the ancestors whose 'desire to be free' was stronger than any force they faced."

To begin with, the 150-year anniversary of the Emancipation Proclamation is noticed, but not a story of note in most people's "Daily Me" or "Filter Bubble". But *The Root* honored the event with a series of articles, infusing the event with significance. Furthermore, a link is drawn between the African Americans who suffered through slavery with the African Americans of the present day.

Commenters in discussion boards also reference ancestors for similar effect. Here, a commenter named Logical Leopard references ancestors and their struggles as a way of shaming modern African Americans into focusing less on the symbolism of racism and focusing more on living up to the examples set by ancestors:

> "I mean, I know that racism is a problem, just like theft is a problem, but we have more recourses to recover from any ill effect of racism than we do against the common thief. So why is that such a big spot on the black agenda, rather than actually bringing up all of our people to a level that our ancestors would be proud of?"[11]

What Logical Leopard is saying is that racism is not the impediment many on the discussion board make it out to be. Blacks are using racism as an excuse. I have not shown the comments to Logical Leopard's post. However, they are a mixture of a minority of people who agree and a majority who disagree. It was a discussion.

I think that comments such as this one by Logical Leopard point to the value of having a space that is by and for a given group—a digital enclave. Most African Americans know that some of the most withering critiques of African Americans come from black people themselves—behind closed doors. But hearing those critiques from someone who shares a similar social position and life experience adds credence to their comments. Whether one agrees or disagrees, one is compelled to consider and address them. This can only happen in black spaces such as barbershops, hair salons, Juke Joints, family get-togethers, and increasingly online.

Being America's Conscious. One way of focusing on the problems in society is through an economic lens. Thus, inequities in educational achievement, for example, are seen to be a matter of unequal funding. Another means of focusing on problems is through a sociopolitical lens. In this case, inequities in who graduates from high school or college are seen as a function of political maneuvering and the changes in education based upon who has authority. The articles and discussions on the *The Root* tend to look at inequality through a moral lens. Continuing with the education example, first one must understand the wrongness and immorality of differential outcomes for social groups, before one delves into policy and economics. Transgressions against African Americans are understood as unjust and immoral. African Americans' experiences as slaves and then living through segregation make them uniquely suited to be, as Melissa Harris-Lacewell (2004) argued, the moral consciousness of America.

For example, the main thrust of an interview done with the new chair of the Congressional Black Caucus, Marcia Fudge, was how the caucus was the "conscience of the Congress"[12]. In this case, the notion that African Americans are the moral standard bearers of the nation is quite explicit. Congresswoman Fudge remarked that the caucus is not just for blacks and that for the caucus "the imperative is to define what is right and then do it".

Or, consider the commenter Black Diaspora responding to a column refuting the theory of "acting white":

"What I see is this: Blacks have been told to fix a problem that they didn't create, and told to do it without the help of those that stood to gain by their not fixing the problem. Until the problems of black America—to the degree that they exist—are seen as America's problems, and not just a black problem, and black children are seen as America's children, and a black future is seen as America's future, the problems that you find vexing will continue and persist. In short, the problems of the black community are not just a black problem, but a national problem, and it will take the whole nation to address those problems and repair what's broken."[13]

The theme of education was prevalent during the month when this analysis was conducted (*The Root* was doing a special series on education). In this passage from an article written by Sherrilyn A. Ifill, president and director-counsel of the NAACP Legal Defense and Educational Fund, we see a combination of the themes of historical context and America's consciousness[14]:

This year marks the 150th anniversary of the Emancipation Proclamation, and the 50th anniversary of the March on Washington. The document and the event were separated by 100 years, but each spoke with equal clarity and urgency to the principles of liberty, equality and opportunity to which we aspire as a nation. There is perhaps no more important institution in keeping us on this path than the public education system. Yet, stark differences in the quality of education available to students of different races persist and *demean* [emphasis added] us all.

The references to the Emancipation Proclamation and the March on Washington are used to evoke the historical struggles and successes of African Americans, and the passage ends by suggesting that the inequities of the nation's educational system are "demeaning" for "us all".

To summarize, the purpose of this content analysis was to explore the conversations on *The Root*. To this end, three themes presented themselves. As a whole, these themes—counterhegemonic interpretations, emphasizing historical context, and being America's moral conscious—work to produce a distinctly African American view of social, cultural, and historical phenomena. In this way *The Root* performs the function of counterpublic.

CONCLUSION

This chapter began by juxtaposing two opposing understandings of deliberative democracy. On the one hand, we have the notion of the public sphere, where public concerns are debated rationally in an open space. On the other hand, we have the notion of numerous counterpublics, where minority and subordinated groups produce their unique dialogues away from spaces populated by the dominant groups in society. These views present opposing designs of what a deliberative democracy should be in modern society. I take these two views, and import them into the digital environment. In the DE, the concept of a networked public sphere mirrors that of a Habermasian public sphere, and the notions of segmentation and polarization mirrors that of counterpublics. I argue that minority groups construct counterpublics in the DE just as they did in the PE. I also argue that because of historical reasons, African Americans may have more incentive to produce a counterpublic in the DE. Given the uniqueness of the digital environment, I decided to term a website that functions like a counterpublic a "digital enclave".

The research presented in this chapter is a case study of one such digital enclave. Network analysis shows that *The Root* is one of a number of African American websites that interconnect disproportionately with similarly themed websites. Further, these websites are at the periphery of a wider network. These websites are in a sense geographically isolated from other websites on the web—similar to the way in which ethnic enclaves are geographically isolated from other parts of a city or white neighborhoods.

Content analysis of the politics section of *The Root* shows that at least three themes present themselves: counterhegemonic interpretations of current events, a reliance upon historical context, and an understanding that African Americans are often the moral conscious of the nation. As a whole, these three themes help construct a uniquely African American discourse, one that is in opposition to mainstream discourse. Thus, both network analysis and content analysis suggests that *The Root* is a digital enclave for African Americans.

Developing digital enclaves is a third digital practice of African Americans. Other racial groups and people of different lifestyles also develop such homogenous spaces. I believe that for African Americans the need for such a space has been greater historically. Further, given the current realities of anti-blackness and the many micro-aggressions endured by African Americans in public, ethnic enclaves such as the *The Root* are indispensable.

The Digital Practice Perspective and Social Policy: Improving the Social, Cultural, and Civic Quality of the Digital Environment

INTRODUCTION

In this chapter, I would like to connect the digital practice perspective to social policy. This will be done in three steps. First, I will review the major legislation that governs the digital environment. These policies are the Telecommunication Act of 1996, the Digital Millennium Copyright Act of 1998, the Federal Communication Commission Policy Statement: Preserving the Free and Open Internet in 2010, and The National Broadband Plan of 2010. During this review a theme will emerge. Policy has been focused on making the digital environment amenable to commerce by increasing the number of businesses (producers) and increasing the number of users (consumers). This is potentially to the detriment of nonmarket spaces where the social, cultural, and civic potential of the digital environment is housed. Second, I will make suggestions for future policy. These suggestions have as their main focus the nurturing of nonmarket spaces in the digital environment. Third, I will show how studies using the digital practice perspective can inform these policies.

SOCIAL POLICY IN THE DIGITAL ENVIRONMENT

The Telecommunications Act of 1996

In *Digital Crossroads*, one of the most thorough explorations of telecommunications policy, Nuechterlein and Weiser (2005) write that the Telecommunications Act of 1996 is "the most important telecommunications legislation – and arguably the most important legislation of any kind – since the New Deal" (p. 69).[1] This act, focused clearly on the infrastructure layer of the digital environment, made it easier for new businesses to enter into the telecommunications market (i.e., selling phone and Internet services to customers).

The act mandated that incumbent companies had to lease their networks to newer competing companies, and that companies had to interconnect with each other.[2] This meant that a newer company providing data or content could use the copper and fiber optic cables—the networks—already in place by larger companies, and further all networks needed to be connected with each other thus allowing all companies to potentially reach most users. Up until this point, businesses could work out arrangements with local and state governments for exclusive telephone rights. The act made these agreements illegal as well, ending the local franchising monopolies that telephone companies enjoyed. The Telecommunications Act of 1996 has indeed ushered in more competition. There are more competing companies in the market (however incumbent companies still dominate the telephone market).[3]

One component of the act stipulates that telecommunications companies must contribute monies towards a universal service fund. This universal service fund would then be used to provide access to telecommunications services to underserved populations. For the everyday citizen, especially citizens who are poor or likely to be in areas where schools and libraries are underfunded, the universal service fund was probably the most important component of this legislation. Monies are funneled into several programs, including a program providing free telephone and mobile phones to low income citizens (Life Line Program) and a program that funds Internet services for schools and libraries (E-Rate Program).[4]

One way of thinking about the Telecommunications Act of 1996 is that it addresses the production (the established telecommunications companies and the newer service providers) and consumption (lower prices for all consumers, and subsidies for lower income consumers) aspects of the digital environment. I see the lenses of the "information society" and the "digital divide" at play here. The digital environment is seen primarily in economic terms (the information society) and the main problem is providing users with access to the goods sold online or providing them with the skills needed to work in the information society (digital divide). The economic emphasis is illustrated in the public remarks made by President Clinton after the signing of the bill:

> "This bill protects consumers against monopolies. It guarantees the diversity of voices our democracy depends upon. Perhaps most of all, it enhances the common good. Under this law, our schools, our libraries, our hospitals will receive telecommunication services at a reduced cost" (Quoted in Dugan and Souza, p. 457).

The use of the phrases "diversity of voices" and "the common good" connotes, if taken out of context, a sense that the bill is primarily focused on increasing the educational, cultural, and civic quality of the digital environment. However, within context, "diversity of voices" means clearly "diversity of Internet subscribers" and "the common good" means "cheaper Internet subscriptions". This is not to say that, ultimately, opening access to the digital environment for producers and consumers does help produce a healthier DE. I believe it does. Indeed, it was the profit motive that produced much of the innovations we now enjoy in the digital environment. However, how much richer the DE could have been if these educational, cultural, and civic dimensions—the "nonmarket" dimensions—were directly addressed at the time of this act?

Digital Millennium Copyright Act of 1998

In 1998 President Clinton signed into law legislation that would "clarify the rights of both the creators and the public in regard to 'documents' created with emerging technologies, such as the web, digital media, and e-books" (Joyce 2002: 54). The Digital Millennium Copyright Act (DMCA) protects intellectual property by outlawing both acts and tools of copyright circumvention. Producers of content employ technologies—primarily embedded code—that prevent the copying or modifying of their products. This is commonly called digital rights management (DRM). However, software can be designed that works around DRM, and allows a consumer to then make copies of that product beyond what is allowed by the original producer. It is these circumvention technologies, used to bypass the DRM of copyrighted materials that are criminalized in this act. Internet service providers (e.g., Verizon or Time Warner), search engines (e.g., Bing or Google), and websites that host content (such as YouTube) are not liable for copyright infringement if they take content down in response to letters from copyright holders. Figure 7.1 shows a Google Transparency Report from February 25, 2014,—a report of the number of sites that have been taken down due to copyright owners reporting copyright infringement since 2011.

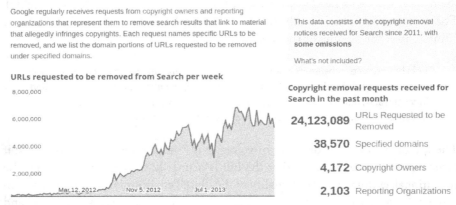

Figure 7.1. Google Transparency Report 2011–February 2014.

In theory, the DMCA is intended to protect all producers of content, from the independent artist selling songs on his personal website to the major recording studies that hold the copyrights to a stable of well-known artists. In practice, it is the large and powerful groups who extract the most benefits from the act if only because they are the most aware of it and have the resources to be most vigilant in its enforcement. Arguably the most famous application of the DMCA was the court case regarding the file-sharing site Napster in the early 2000s. Napster allowed users to share copyrighted material (mainly songs) with other users. Napster was sued by the Recording Industry Artists of America, found guilty of copyright infringement, and was forced to shut down its file sharing service.

A more recent application of the DMCA concerns the unlocking of mobile phones. When a mobile phone is bought, it is usually configured to operate only on the service provider it was bought from. If a customer wishes to change providers, she will not be able to use the device she had bought on another provider's network. In other words, if I buy a mobile phone through AT&T, I cannot, after my service contract has expired, keep my phone and move to another network provider such as T-Mobile. This "locking" is, as with most things, a matter of coding. Each mobile phone comes with a Subscriber Identity Module (SIM), the memory chip with a user's unique information. The SIM carries, among other things, your plan information and phone number. The network provider has installed software on the SIM card that connects an ID given to the customer and the serial number of that particular phone. If a customer tries to use a SIM card from another provider, the phone will not work. Before the 26th of January 2013, customers had been able to "unlock" their phones legally because of an exemption written into the DMCA. However, the cell phone industry has argued that this is a violation of copyright, and in January of 2013, the Librarian of Congress agreed.[5]

The case of Napster vs. the RIAA and the mobile phone unlocking ban are mentioned here to illustrate a general point—the DMCA has wide-ranging consequences in the digital environment because it can restrict one of the properties that make the DE special. Recall that one of the properties of the DE is that the costs of manipulating content are lowered (see Chapter 3). This manipulating includes the production, dissemination, reproduction, modifying, and copying of digitized symbolic content. The DMCA clearly hinders this manipulation and as a consequence impedes the full potential of what people and groups can accomplish. While copyright protections are important in order to spur innovations, the way in which the DMCA is currently interpreted and enforced reduces the DE to a place of commerce—sellers and buyers of copyrighted products.

Federal Communication Commission Policy Statement: Preserving the Free and Open Internet in 2010

Here is Columbia law professor Tim Wu (2003) defining the concept of network neutrality on his webpage:

> "Network neutrality is best defined as a network design principle. The idea is that a maximally useful public information network aspires to treat all content, sites, and platforms equally. This allows the network to carry every form of information and support every kind of application."[6]

Wu coined the term network neutrality in his 2003 article "Network Neutrality, Broadband Discrimination". Wu's phrase "carry every form of information and support every kind of application" refers to the fact that, if service providers could discriminate, they would inevitably favor their own content, or a favored third party. If this should happen, then large content providers could, through agreements with service providers or by simply paying whatever fees service providers charge, crowd out the market and choke innovation.

Wu is widely credited with articulating and popularizing the idea that access to network services should be given universally and without discrimination. However, network neutrality is a fundamental aspect of the original design of the Internet. The Internet is designed as an end-to-end structure, such that the use or application of data traveling through a network is done by the end users themselves, and not intermediary hosts. In a simple example, suppose I send a photo through my computer to a friend. The data I send through the network to my friend's computer is not interpreted or manipulated by the service provider. It is the applications on my computer (e-mail, photo editing software) and the applications on my friend's computer that interpret and manipulate the data. All communications via the Internet were designed originally to take on this end-to-end character.

Kimball's (2013) essay on the discourse of network neutrality chronicles the move of this principle from its origination in the computer engineering community, to online content providers such as Google, to public interest groups such as Free Press. As calls for network neutrality grew louder, network operators such as Verizon and Comcast formed an opposition arguing that network neutrality rules were a type of overregulation. In the end, the primary players were corporate interests, with Google carrying the mantle of network neutrality and network operators pushing for more freedom managing their networks. Kimball argues that as different groups took on the cause of network neutrality and battle lines were drawn, the public meaning of network neutrality changed:

> "The 'net neutrality' that gained traction in the policy sphere by 2010 was a very loosely translated version of the principle – the result of several levels of compromise between Google (representing online services) and Verizon (representing network operators), with little input from legal and technological experts or public interest groups…while the principle solidified discursively, the embodiment of the principle in policy became significantly diluted" (34–35).

By the time network neutrality principles were officially adopted by the FCC, the label used to define these principles, and as Kimball argues the ideas themselves, had deviated significantly from their original meaning.

This new meaning was codified in the FCC policy statement "Preserving the Free and Open Internet". The policy statement lists three broad rules[7]:

1. Transparency. Broadband providers must disclose information regarding their network management practices, performance, and the commercial terms of their broadband services.
2. No blocking. Fixed broadband providers (such as DSL, cable modem, or fixed wireless providers) may not block lawful content, applications, services, or non-harmful devices. Mobile broadband providers may not block lawful websites, or applications that compete with their voice or video telephony services.
3. No unreasonable discrimination. Fixed broadband providers may not unreasonably discriminate in transmitting lawful network traffic over a consumer's broadband Internet access service. Unreasonable discrimination of network traffic could take the form of particular services or websites appearing slower or degraded in quality.

These rules provide some protections in that service providers must be forthright with their customers in their network management practices, and any alterations in service must be "reasonable". Under no circumstances can legal content be blocked (illegal content such as child pornography or content that has been copied unlawfully can be blocked). Also, "commercial arrangements between a broadband provider and a third party such as a content or applications provider to favor some traffic over other traffic in the broadband connection to a subscriber of the broadband provider—are unlikely to satisfy the 'no unreasonable discrimination' standard" (Baker et al. 2011). This helps businesses in the software and application layers compete on a level playing field. As I mentioned earlier, larger corporations like Amazon or Netflix could pay for faster service download speeds, creating a two-tiered network and severally hampering small businesses' efforts to compete.

These rules deviate from the original intent of network neutrality in at least three instances. First, while mobile broadband providers are a part of the digital environment, they are given more leeway—the open Internet rules are far less restrictive for mobile broadband providers. Second, similar to cable subscriptions, end users can pay for priority service and this is not considered unreasonable discrimination. In other words, an end user can pay more per month for faster download speeds and a larger allotment of downloadable data. Third, fixed broadband providers (usually your home Internet connection) cannot block content, but they can slow your Internet speed if it is "reasonable".

In Figure 7.2, I show the Open Internet rules in action. In May of 2013, my Internet service provider sent me an e-mail saying that I had gone over a predetermined allotment of data and that my network experience could be improved by, as is written in the e-mail, "moving to a package featuring faster downloads and larger data usage allowance". My ISP had been transparent by sending me an e-mail and was warning me that they would have to do some "network management" to maintain the quality of the network. They suggested that I should pay more in order to avoid this network management. Baker et al. (2011) write "The prohibition against unreasonable discrimination does not bar reasonable network management to address network congestion or service quality issues as may arise, for example, at usage peaks or if heavy users threaten to crowd out others" (298). Thus, my guess is that should my data usage move significantly past my allotment, my content will not be blocked, but my download speeds will be slowed (reasonable discrimination).

-------- Original message --------
From: "Cox Internet Support Team (no reply)" <noreply@cox.net>
Date: 08/09/2013 10:07 AM (GMT-05:00)
To:
Subject: Overage Notification on your Cox High Speed Internet package

Dear Roderick Graham,

We have provided notice to you recently regarding your monthly data usage allowance, and as a reminder your current Cox High Speed Internet package includes 100 Gigabytes of data usage. As of August 08, 2013, your household has used 106 Gigabytes of data in the current billing cycle, which exceeds your plan amount for the current month.

Remember that you can view your data usage by logging into your account and checking your data usage meter in Internet Tools:
https://myaccount.cox.net/internettools/datausage/usage.cox

Based on your usage needs, your online experience would be improved by moving to a package featuring even faster download speeds and a larger data usage allowance. To learn about special offers for all package levels, call us at 1-877-840-2777 for assistance in selecting the option that best fits your household's needs.

If you're interested in learning more about data usage and the factors affecting it please visit:
http://www.cox.com/DataUsage

Some common factors affecting data usage include the number of Internet-connected devices in the household, Wi-Fi network security, the amount of streaming video watched, and the presence of viruses and spyware on one or more home computers. We strongly encourage you to check your Home Networking security today in Internet Tools and secure your network:
https://myaccount.cox.net/internettools/homenetworking/homenetworking.cox

Thanks again for choosing Cox High Speed Internet.

Sincerely,

Cox High Speed Internet Team

Figure 7.2.   Example of Reasonable Discrimination.

The FCC's Open Internet policy statement is a classic example of a political compromise that pleases no one. Public advocacy groups are unhappy with the tremendous leeway network operators have in discriminating content, and network operators are displeased that they cannot manage their network as they see fit.

At this point a pattern should be emerging. The federal government is keenly interested in the DE as a business environment, and has been fairly diligent in its protection of competition and user access (with user access being understood as being able to afford Internet or mobile phone service).

But the federal government should take a stronger interest in the nonmarket aspects of the DE as they relate to network neutrality. A subscriber to a network should be able to pay one flat rate for the same service. Network operators may argue that hindering "network management" and not allowing content providers to pay for faster services interferes with the free market. I am inclined to agree. Unfortunately (or fortunately) the Internet is *not* an entertainment service like cable. The Internet is far more than an entertainment or even an information service where content is merely bought and sold. While the market aspect of the DE takes center stage, it is the nonmarket aspects that make the technology revolutionary, and should be regulated as such.

The National Broadband Plan of 2010

In 2009, with the American economy mired in a recession, President Obama signed into law the American Recovery and Reinvestment Act. The law, more commonly known as "the stimulus", was an $800 billion package of government spending designed to kick-start an economic recovery. As a part of the stimulus package $7.2 billion was set aside for achieving the main (but not only) goal of providing universal access of broadband Internet service to American citizens. The FCC was given a mandate to come up with a plan to reach this goal. In March of 2010, the FCC produced the National Broadband Plan.[8]

The plan is broad in scope and is composed of over 250 specific recommendations that are to be carried out over the next several years. The recommendations within the plan can be divided into three parts. The first part, "innovation and investment", involves building infrastructure and increasing competition between telecommunications providers. The second part, "inclusion", involves increasing the affordability and availability of broadband to unserved and underserved communities. Notably, the Universal Service Fund, first mandated in the '96 Telecommunications Act, has been reconfigured to provide incentives for the private sector to build infrastructure in rural areas. The third part, "national purposes", involves applying the benefits of broadband to the nation's institutions, including hospitals, schools, and government.

The media's response has been to focus on what the plan means for the economy. In most newspaper reports, the lead has been the immediate impact to individual Internet subscribers. The plan has a goal of delivering 100Mbps access to 100 million users by 2020.[9] This is then followed with questions of how the government and businesses will achieve this goal, and how the goal will help or hurt the job prospects of the individual users. Thus, in a discussion of the plan in *Information Today*, the author writes:

> "The FCC's plan considers fostering competition as a solution [to low adoption rates]. Now, more than three-quarters of all households have only two broadband providers to choose from and many rural areas have only one. The FCCs research found that areas with more competition offered lower prices, more choices, and faster connection speeds. This emphasis on competition was good news to Gerald R. Faulhaber, professor emeritus of business and public policy at the University of Pennsylvania. Faulhaber, who also participated in the FCC's working groups for the plan, argues that competition – not regulation or service mandates – is the key to access." (Schiller, Kurt, 2010. "A Simple Plan: Broadband and the FCC." *Information Today* 27(7):1–43)

Similarly, in response to a 2010 poll showing that Americans cared little about broadband, an FCC spokesperson responded by clarifying the economic gains:

> "Federal officials said the report does not undercut the administration's effort, but instead shows the need for educating people about the importance of broadband technology for access to information on healthcare, education and jobs. 'Today's Pew

report confirms what the FCC found in our broadband survey last year: There are still too many barriers to broadband adoption in America,' said FCC spokeswoman Jen Howard. 'That's why the National Broadband Plan lays out a strategy for improving digital literacy and ensuring that all Americans can take full advantage of the benefits of broadband.' The FCC estimates that if all homes had broadband, corporations would save $500 billion over 15 years from the use of electronic health records instead of paper. It also projects that $1.2 billion could be saved by video consultations between doctors and patients in cases where office visits are not practical." (*Washington Post*, Support for broadband loses speed; Blacks gain more access Older Americans question benefit, Cecilia Kang, Pg. A10)

This emphasis by the media on the economic, as opposed to the social or cultural aspects of broadband is understandable. The plan was written in the context of a recession and the administration's attempts to reinvigorate the economy.

The plan is quite comprehensive, and is an improvement over the '96 telecommunications act. Within the "inclusion" portion of the plan is a call for a digital literacy corps to conduct training and perform outreach to groups that are reluctant to adopt broadband. The "national purposes" portion of the plan makes several recommendations for fully integrating our nation's institutions into the DE. For example, recommendations are made to increase the use of e-health, online education, a national public safety system for first responders, and increasing funding for digital public media.

Ultimately, the FCC's recommendations are just that. The process through which these recommendations become actualized through government agencies relies on the approval of specific actions and the success of government agencies carrying them out. At the time of this writing, the early emphasis has been on the practical matters of collecting data. The universal service fund has also been redesigned and implemented. Only time will tell if the nonmarket recommendations come to fruition.

SOCIAL POLICY, NONMARKET SPACES, AND THE DIGITAL PRACTICE PERSPECTIVE

The previous paragraphs show how government action vis-à-vis the digital environment has been oriented towards the market. In this section I list three recommendations for social policy going forward. For each I discuss how studies using the digital practice perspective can inform an implementation of each recommendation. These recommendations rest upon an assumption about what is the *most desirable* digital environment for a nation. I assume that ultimately what will produce a healthy, stable digital environment are policies that produce a nonmarket space that is at *least* as robust as the current market space. What I mean by non-market spaces are software, websites, mobile applications, and content that are not produced for, or predicated on, economic exchanges.

Individuals cannot nor should not rely on businesses and corporations to give them the most enriching digital environment experience. Consider the use of Facebook for publicizing one's group, cause, or event. Using Facebook is probably the best way to make your cause known. Facebook has the largest amount of users and its integration into so many elements of both the physical and digital environments—think of the numerous software applications that by design allow one to connect through Facebook, or the fact that almost every institution and company has their own Facebook page. So as of today creating a group page on Facebook is an optimal way of publicizing one's group, cause, or event. But it is not completely certain that the "free service" that Facebook offers will remain so. Facebook will find ever more ways to extract profit from their services. When this happens, it will necessarily lead to lower income groups being excluded. This is not completely out of the realm of possibility. As I write a draft of this chapter, YouTube—an optimal means of getting one's video content out to the public—has introduced several new pay channels. As another example, consider the vibrant counterpublic of African Americans (Chapter 6). This counterpublic performs a vital function for African Americans. However, the website I focused on, *The Root*, is a commercial enterprise. As long as it relies on the market it will always be vulnerable to the whims of that market. Businesses may pull ads if the content does not suit their tastes, or the website may have to modify its content to fit the trends of the marketplace. The only way that groups can counteract this is by producing their own spaces that are not beholden to market logic.

Currently, market spaces dominate the digital environment. A look at the top websites on Alexa.Com shows that only one of the top 20 American-based websites is a nonmarket one, Wikipedia.[10] Another way of thinking about this is that at each layer of the DE, market alternatives dominate nonmarket ones. Netflix and YouTube dominate the content layers of the digital environment. Both are market alternatives. Netflix is more obvious because it charges customers up front for their services. But YouTube is also a commodified space. We are lured in by the free videos, but to watch those videos we are subject to a barrage of advertisements. At the application layer, websites like Twitter, Facebook, and Google search clearly dominate. Like YouTube, their market nature is not glaringly obvious, but ads run down the sides of screens, and some content and services must be purchased. At the software layers, where there are clearly viable nonmarket alternatives (open source software), there is still domination by market-based software. Thus, the most popular operating systems are Windows and Mac OS (although Linux is often viewed as a better alternative) and arguably the most popular statistical software is SPSS (although R is often viewed as a better alternative, a claim I can vouch for). At the hardware and infrastructure layers government has maintained a fairly hands-off approach, although it has at times assisted citizens in the purchasing of hardware and either assisted or subsidized the building of infrastructure.

This is in stark contrast to the initial development of the digital environment, where government and educational institutions were heavily involved (see Curran 2012; Hafner and Lyon 1996). In terms of years, the Internet has spent more than half of its lifetime as a nonmarket space, as it was under government control and run by universities from 1969 when the first data was sent between two computers, to 1991 when commercial enterprises were allowed online. Even after ".com" websites were allowed online, it still took some time for commerce to grow, spurred on, as James Curran (2012) writes, by the adoption of a standard protocol for credit cards in 1997. By the late 1990s the writing was on the wall. Curran (2012) describes what people feared would come to pass:

> "These developments [early endeavors by businesses to generate profits online] were viewed by some as a portent of things to come. They indicated that what had once been a largely pre-market space in which content was freely distributed and available to all online could be transformed into a commodified space where selling and advertising became prominent, fees only websites proliferated at the expense of the web's open access 'commons', and net neutrality was terminated in order to make way for the creation of fast Internet service for the affluent (and a slow one for budget citizens)" (p. 43).

There is room for both market as well as nonmarket enterprises. The digital environment is large enough to accommodate both spaces. But care has to be taken so that the digital environment does not become completely commodified. The purpose of these recommendations is to maintain the freedom necessary for the growth of nonmarket spaces, educate the population in digital literacy and the merits of maintaining a nonmarket space, and provide incentives for social groups to develop nonmarket spaces that are in tune with their historical and cultural needs from the physical environment.

Keep the Internet Open

First, and most importantly, the Internet needs to remain open and possibly be *more* open. This will allow individuals more freedom to explore the DE and leverage its properties. US policy has been schizophrenic on this issue, at one end the FCC proclaims it will enforce an open Internet and the freedom of users to download content without discrimination, yet on the other end the enforcement of the DMCA by the Librarian of Congress means that users cannot unlock the phones they purchased and use them as they see fit. This is not an issue without nuance. Businesses have a right to extract as much profit from their enterprise as possible. Indeed, it is the profit motive that will continue to produce the rapid innovations we enjoy. However, rampant profit seeking often conflicts with the needs of the public as a whole, and the balance of power is clearly moving in the direction of business. As mentioned above, net neutrality rules are quite soft for landline broadband, and almost nonexistent for wireless companies. Furthermore, tiered pricing plans are allowable and are now the standard. This is a wide departure from the spirit of net neutrality, and very regrettable.

Scholars are aware of the importance of an open Internet. Some of the more notable scholars and their works include Yochai Benkler's (2007) *The Wealth of Networks: How Social Production Transforms Markets and Freedom*, Johnathan Zittrain's (2008) *The Future of the Internet and How to Stop It*, Peter Suber's (2012) *Open Access*, and Julie Cohen's (2012) *Configuring the Networked Self: Law, Code, and the Play of Everyday Practice*. These works, from different angles, develop cogent arguments in favor of maintaining the Open Internet.

There is also a strong and vocal group of digital environment users who consume these books and understand the arguments posed. This group also reads magazines such as *Wired* and *PCWorld*. They are active in organizations such as The Electronic Frontier Foundation and The Internet Society. This collection of authors, scholars, lawyers, and the institutions they support are almost universally in support of the Free and Open Internet Movement. Let's call them the digerati.[11] The digerati have done quite well in generating opposition to the Stop Online Piracy Act (SOPA) and the Protect Intellectual Property Act (PIPA) and eventually preventing those bills from moving through congress. Those bills, aimed at foreign websites that infringe on copyrighted material, had the side effect of reducing Internet freedom. These groups were aware of this, and their online petitions, op-ed pieces, and public advocacy groups put tremendous pressure on lawmakers.

I suspect that the digerati are, by and large, "WEIRD"—White Educated Industrialized Rich and Democratic.[12] They are outliers, coming from a specific race, class, and national background that determine to a great extent what they see as important in the digital environment. Their uniqueness does not invalidate their motives or goals (of which I share). It does suggest that it may take more than the legal-rational arguments in the books listed above or an emphasis on the technological freedom the Open Internet allows to generate a *mass* interest in preserving an Open Internet. Take Johnathan Zittrain's (2008) argument in *The Future of the Internet and How to Stop It*. Zittrain argues that the bundling of closed software into appliances— for example, the Netflix software found in a television set or DVD player—is restricting the openness of the Internet. One cannot modify the code in these devices, nor can one use different software. This is absolutely spot on. But my guess is that the average citizen (as he himself points out) finds these tethered devices convenient and secure, and cares nothing for the potential to code or modify the software.

This is where studies generated by the digital practice perspective come into play. *Studies using the digital practice perspective can inform policy makers and the public at large by providing empirical evidence for the importance of an Open Internet in the everyday lives of people.* In this book, I presented three studies that show how African Americans are using the digital environment to reach their goals. These goals can be quotidian (keeping in touch with family), they can be ways to overcome some entrenched historical disadvantages (lack of weak ties across class and racial lines), and they can be very empowering (the formation of a counterpublic). Studies of other groups—from Hispanics to Tea Partiers to gay men to Thai housewives—will inevitably reveal the ways these groups leverage the DE to reach their needs. Showing how important the DE is on the everyday level can help gin up support for the Free and Open Internet Movement. If the digital environment is seen as fundamental to the social, civic, educational and cultural well-being of people, then strict copyright policies, tiered pricing, and other mechanisms businesses use to increase profit and stifle user freedom will be seen as unjust.

Emphasizing Digital Literacy (or Digital Environment Literacy) in Public Education

The second way in which government can produce a healthy digital environment is by encouraging the teaching of digital literacy in classrooms from K – 12 to colleges and universities. The type of digital literacy I am imagining takes a holistic view of the digital environment. This means teaching both market skills (e.g., specific job skills using computers, applying for jobs using computers, etc.) *and* nonmarket skills (e.g., learning how to use the DE to become an active citizen, Internet etiquette, learning about open source alternatives, etc.).

The distortions of the information society and the digital divide have impeded the progress of holistic digital literacy in education. Digital literacy, when taught to children, is seen not as a liberal arts or general studies course designed to make them democratically engaged citizens, but more as vocational one—teaching them basic "how to" skills. When digital literacy is taught to adults, its primary purpose is to prepare adults for applying for jobs online or teaching basic computer skills for the world of work. For example, the FCC has partnered with the nonprofit organization Connect2Compete to offer job-focused digital literacy classes. The press release on the FCC's broadband website reads:

"The fact that 66 million Americans are without basic digital literacy skills, the skill-set needed to use a computer and the Internet, is troubling both for job seekers and employers alike. In fact, 52% of American employers are experiencing difficulty filling mission-critical positions, up from 14% in 2010, due to the nationwide skills gap.

As the costs of digital exclusion rises, what's at stake is not only the competitiveness of the American workforce, but also the vitality of our country in the 21st century. The good news is the private sector, government, and philanthropy are working together, through the Connect2Compete (C2C) coalition, to help close the digital divide and the skills gap" (Usdan and Almasy 2012).

This is all well and good. But the digital environment is more than this, and digital literacy programs should take this into account. The same way that an understanding of traffic patterns:

> *"The red light means stop,*
> *The green light means go,*
> *And the yellow light means be careful*
> *These are three things I know..."*

And how the government works

> *"I'm just a bill*
> *Yes I'm only a bill*
> *And I'm sittin' here on Capitol Hill..."*

were seen as essential education for children, so should an understanding of the DE. Citizens need to be aware of the capabilities of the digital environment, as well as their rights and privileges in it.

We already have some knowledge about what people know and do not know. Indeed, scholars' attention on a second digital divide, as discussed in Chapter 2, is about a divide in skills, which can often be interpreted as a divide in digital literacy. For example, the Web Use Project, based in Northwestern University's Department of Communication Studies and led by Communication Professor Eszter Hargittai, produces studies on how people in their everyday lives use the Internet.[13] One strand of research within the Web Use Project focuses on measuring Internet literacy (Hargittai 2005; Hargittai 2009; Hargittai and Hsieh 2012) and differences in the Internet competencies between groups (Hargittai and Hinnant 2008). A survey instrument developed to measure differences in Internet literacy, despite rapid changes in technology, has proven reliable over several years (Hargittai and Hsieh 2012). Some of the questions on the survey are shown in Table 7.1 (from

Hargittai 2009). These types of studies are important and necessary, especially when one needs to zero in on specific Internet skills for the world of work.

Table 7.1*. Web Use Project Sample Survey Questions

The Survey Administered by the Web Use Project starts with this prompt:
"How familiar are you with the following computer and Internet-related items? Please choose a number between 1 and 5, where 1 represents no understanding and 5 represents full understanding of the item."
Some of the computer and Internet-related items are:

- JPEG
- Frames
- Preference settings
- Newsgroups

- Wiki
- Malware
- Social bookmarking
- Podcasting

*reproduced from Hargittai (2009)

While the survey instrument developed by the Web Use Project, along with other surveys,[14] gives us some understanding of the differences in types of digital environment literacy (mainly Internet literacy), the links between this knowledge and its application within the everyday lives of people are not always clear. How much does it matter if someone is aware of the term JPEG? If one is oriented towards the world of work, then having an academic understanding of these terms and how they are interrelated is essential. However, if one is oriented towards understanding the use of the DE in the everyday lives of people, then being able to recall the meaning of this term is irrelevant.

Studies using the digital practice perspective can show us what are the most essential competencies needed in order to be a productive citizen in the digital environment. They can also show us, by looking at what groups do in the digital environment, what are the key gaps in knowledge. How much do students know about their digital footprint? Do they know what ".gov", ".com", and ".org" signify, and how a website gets those designations? Then, courses in K – 12, and liberal arts courses in college, can focus on making students aware of the capabilities of the DE and what they can and cannot do in it.

Incentivizing Nonmarket Spaces

Government should provide incentives for the development of nonmarket spaces in the digital environment. Incentives can be given to individuals or non-profits pledging to produce public spaces at any level of the DE. As discussed earlier in this book, the digital environment provides new leverage for old behaviors. No group is more familiar with their behaviors in the physical environment than the groups themselves, and no group knows how to best use the digital environment to meet their needs than the groups themselves. With an Open Internet and a solid educational base (the previous two recommendations), incentives could be the catalyst for groups to produce their own unique nonmarket spaces.

Government already provides assistance to groups in several ways. Since the Telecommunications Act of 1996, government has subsidized Internet service in lower income schools and libraries through the E-Rate program. Government has provided subsidies for network service providers to expand their networks into low density rural areas. Government agencies have also made funding available for the teaching of digital literacy—generally to adults. These are designed to provide access to underserved groups and preparing adults for the digital economy.

Government does not, however, provide the incentives and support needed for groups to build more robust and stable nonmarket, public spaces in the digital environment themselves. The types of incentives needed would amount to providing funding for domain registration, Internet subscription, storage space, and possibly consulting—all of the things needed for a private company to enter into the digital environment. It may also amount to funding a database or clearinghouse for blocks of code for websites, open source software, and mobile applications. Other options could include providing tax breaks for owners and operators of websites that serve the public or communities.

CONCLUSION

Our understanding of the digital environment is seen through the lenses of the information society (read: the Internet and other new technologies are primarily economic entities) and the digital divide (read: the digital environment is about access to the technology being sold and the development of the skills needed to perform in the information society). Theses lenses cause us to view the DE as a world of producers and consumers. The review in this chapter of federal telecommunications policy over the last two decades supports this conclusion. Policy has had as a main focus the increasing of competition between producers and the increasing of access for consumers.

Social policy has neglected the nonmarket aspect of the digital environment. The policy recommendations I list are aimed at redressing this oversight. First and foremost, the Internet needs to remain open and free—network neutrality rules need to be enforced much more vigorously than they currently are.

Second, digital literacy in schools needs to take a more holistic approach. Instead of the current narrow focus on teaching skills for the information economy, people should be taught how to navigate the DE as active citizens. Finally, government should incentivize the growth of nonmarket spaces at every layer of the DE through subsidies and tax cuts. Studies that apply a digital practice perspective can help with these policy goals by providing a greater understanding of what groups do in the DE in their everyday lives.

Conclusion: Smart Mobs, Flash Mobs, Flash Robs and the Revolutionary Potential of the Digital Environment

Of all the writers and theorists of the Information Society, Howard Rheingold is one of the most prescient, spotting social trends where others see only bits and bytes. In *Smart Mobs*, Rheingold (2003) described how mobile technology was providing new leverage for the natural human tendency to form groups and co-operate. In Rheingold's words, mobile technologies *"enable people to act together in new ways and in situations where collective action was not possible before* [emphasis in original]." (xviii)

Rheingold describes various instances where groups of people used mobile phones to work together in pursuit of a common goal. He called these mobile collectivities "smart mobs". An example he gives is the ousting of former president of the Philippines Joseph Estrada:

> "On January 20, 2001, President Joseph Estrada of the Philippines became the first head of state in history to lose power to a smart mob. Tens of thousands of Filipinos converged on Epifanio de los Santas Avenue, known as 'Edsa,' within an hour of the first text message volleys: 'Go 2EDSA, Wear blck.' Over four days, more than a million citizens showed up, mostly dressed in black. Estrada fell." (157–158)

Rheingold notes several other instances of smart mobs, from the "critical mass" bicycle demonstrations held in various cities around the world, to the World

Trade Organization demonstrations held in 1999 (commonly called the "Battle of Seattle").

A smart mob does not need to be a political or social movement, however. In the summer of 2003 Bill Wasik[1], an editor of the popular technology magazine *Wired*, sent an e-mail to friends asking them to meet in public places and perform nonsensical acts. He called this collection of people simply a "MOB". The first e-mail began:

> "You are invited to take part in MOB, the project that creates an inexplicable mob of people in New York City for ten minutes or less. Please forward this to other people you know who might like to join."

Wasik asked those receiving the e-mail, in fairly detailed instructions, to assemble at 7:24, walk towards the clothier Claire's Accessories from different routes depending upon their birthday, and meet inside the store, "keeping chatter to a minimum". If approached by a salesperson, members of the MOB should reply that they are just looking and that they heard a mob was going to be there. For those who could not get into the store because it was too crowded, they should mass around the front of the store and yell or chant "depending on the vibe", Wasik wrote. At 7:31, when the alarms begin to beep, everyone should leave. No one, Wasik urged, should stay after 7:33. This first attempt at organizing a mob was not successful. Someone had leaked the upcoming event to the police, and they were waiting.

While organizing his second attempt at a MOB, Wasik wrote about the cause of the first MOB's failure:

> "I am thinking, in particular, of whoever saw it necessary to tell the store and/or the police department about MOB #1, causing SIX POLICE OFFICERS AND A PADDYWAGON to be sent out to disrupt it. Let us call this person 'Squealy'.

Learning from past experiences, Wasik gave only limited information via e-mail, and arranged for a confederate to meet members of the mob and give more information. Like the first mob, actions were coordinated relatively precisely. MOBers were to meet in one of four locations based upon their birth, where they would wait until one of Wasik's confederates came to provide more detailed information about where the entire mob would meet. The second mob was successful, as more than 100 people met around a rug on the ninth floor of Macy's.

These collectives, micro-coordinated through information and communication technologies (ICTs), are better known now as "flash mobs". Much has changed since Wasik's first flash mobs. For one, Wasik was organizing at a time when social networking sites were still in a gestation period. Wasik used e-mails to organize his flash mobs. At this point e-mail is a dinosaur for many young people. Flash mobs are organized via Facebook, Twitter, and text messaging. Also, many of the early flash mobbers—and especially those that were a part of Wasik's original group—were white, educated, from industrialized countries and from Western countries (the same WEIRDs from Chapter 7). But the class, race, and geographic profiles of flash mob participants have broadened. One can go onto YouTube and see several videos of flash mobs in Singapore, Sydney, Australia, Toronto, and London.

Some of the more recent flash mobs are faithful to Wasik's original idea and ethos only on the surface. For these mobs, the nonsensical acts of Wasik's original MOB are, well, nonsensical. The purpose of a flash mob for these groups has a practical purpose. In Wales, a group of visually impaired youth danced in a flash mob. The mob was for the promotion of a non-profit organization that assists visually impaired youth and their parents (McWatt 2011). There was less spontaneity here. An organizer for the event said "Everyone worked so hard practising the routine during weeks leading up to the performance and it was worth it because they were all brilliant on the day." Practicing before the performance, and using the mob as a means to promote a cause moves the Wales mob away from Wasik's. Similarly, Samoans in New Zealand, organized through Facebook and text messages, assembled in downtown Wellington, New Zealand, to sing songs of support for their national rugby team during the 2011 rugby world cup matches (*New Zealand Herald*, 2011).

These examples – from those cited by Rheingold, to Wasik's flash mobs, to the examples from Wales and New Zealand—show us ways that groups have leveraged information and communication technologies (ICTs) in the Information Society. From protesting a government, to supporting a football team, to doing nothing in particular, we see the diversity of group behavior in the Information Society. Across the globe, individuals and groups have found ways to use new technology to their benefit. Wherever we see a sufficient number of ICTs, there will be some sort of smart mobbing. Even in China, where organizing for anti-government protests is prohibited, flash mobbing has manifested itself in "team buying", where strangers who met online meet in a store and demand discounts (Montlake 2006). This is the power of the digital environment.

One group in the United States, long considered disadvantaged in the Information Society, has also leveraged ICTs to achieve their goals. Only these goals are more dubious. Many major cities in the United States have had to grapple with the "smart" organizing of street crime. Young minorities from urban environments were using Facebook and Twitter to coordinate deviant and illegal activity. These youngsters communicated via Twitter or Facebook on mobile Internet connections, coordinated their behaviors, and physically overwhelmed or tactically outmaneuvered those less coordinated. They swarmed stores, stealing merchandise by working together quickly. With several people all stealing merchandise at once, store owners were powerless to stop them. *The flash mobs had morphed into flash robs.*

In most cases, flash robs are non-violent. However, the flash robs that result in physical confrontations make the most headlines. On one summer day in late July of 2011 in Chicago, five people were attacked and robbed in what were called "flash mob robberies" (Janssen and Rozek 2011). The teens, working in small groups, surrounded their victims, physically assaulted them, and stole their valuables. iPads, bikes, and wallets were stolen. There was some redemption for the victims in this particular incident, as they were able to identify some of the attackers in a police lineup.

Several urban areas such as Las Vegas, Philadelphia, and Washington, D.C., have suffered through outbreaks of flash robs. They had become such a public concern in the Washington, D.C., area that officials in Montgomery County, a county in Maryland, proposed a bill that would impose tougher penalties on those involved in flash robs (Noble 2011). The most attention has come from flash robs in Philadelphia. Flash robs there had grown continuingly larger and more brazen. In 2009, police rushed to stop what they called "a rampage by more than 100 who blocked traffic, pounded on cars, stole merchandise, and assaulted several people" in an upscale area of Philadelphia (Slobodzian 2009). By March of the following year, officials were considering an early youth curfew as thousands of youth swarmed the streets (Wood and Kerstra 2010). By early August 2011, Philadelphia had enacted an early curfew on anyone under the age of 18 in select areas of the city (Graham 2011).

At the time of this writing, Philadelphia officials seem to have gotten flash robs under control. But these crimes continue to crop up around the country. Here is an ABC news story posted within the week of my writing this chapter in late 2013. The story begins by describing flash robberies in Chicago:

> "They are stealing racks of coats…it's over in less than 30 seconds. They're not done. The same thieves are believed to have targeted two other sports authority stores, this week alone. Police are seeing crimes like this around the country. So called flash robs. Coordinated groups of thieves, who swarm stores…. In some cases the theft is loud and crazy, like at this Florida Walmart. In others, it's stunningly calm."[2]

These are street crimes that hurt the individual victims and tear at the moral fabric of those communities. They should be dealt with accordingly. The perpetrators of these crimes should face some type of recriminations for their actions, and steps should be taken to curtail future transgressions.

But there is something to be learned here. These flash robberies were damned hard to pull off! These youths managed to merge cultural precedents, structural conditions, and technological affordances into a shockingly effective digital practice. They were able to participate in collective action, even in the face of serious punishment. Those who study collective behavior are aware of how uncommon this is. I'm not trying to glamorize flash robberies. To be sure, this is a moral setback with respect to the laws of the physical environment. But I can clearly see how this is a social triumph with respect to the use of ICTs and the digital environment. Studying how these youths were able to manage such a feat—the values, norms, and social structures of their everyday lives and how they interact with the affordances of ICTs—may provide community leaders insight into how they can organize these youths for more proper ends.

The accomplishments of these young men can even provide insight for people in other walks of life. Why must protests be a lurching column of people chanting "No Justice No Peace" ? This may have worked in the age of television and the age of Main Street, where everyone went to a central area to shop, protests could clog that area, the evening news could cover it, and everyone would see it. But the central downtown shopping areas of cities—although making a comeback—have lost their economic and social significance, and people are not watching the evening news as much as they used to. Moreover, these large protests require some degree of planning, and law enforcement and city officials inevitably get involved. Barricades are put up. Traffic is rerouted. Marches, with pre-planned origins and destinations, are guided by police standing around at strategic points. The manifest function of these steps is to ensure the safety of all involved, but the latent functions are to control the march, sanitize it, and turn it into a parade.

But what about organizing several clusters of people, not to flash rob, but to *flash protest?* You can have small groups of twenty to forty people, showing up in different areas of a city, waiting until a coordinated point in time, and then breaking out in a peaceful protest. People in the group can video the rally and post it to YouTube. When police come to break it up, this too can be recorded. Given their size, it would be quite easy for a given rally to dissolve, and using the power of ICTs, communicate on a new place to reform and begin the process again. If the purpose of protests is to raise awareness and express public dissatisfaction with a given policy, this method may be far more effective than the traditional march down Main Street.

The purpose of *The Digital Practices of African Americans: An Approach to Studying Cultural Change in the Information Society* was to make it easier for us to see these social accomplishments and the possibilities that lie in them. As I said in the introduction to this book, the impetus for this work came from a frustration I had with finding academic commentary on the social transformations brought on by the Information Society. I saw this dearth of literature as a consequence of how we see ICTs. Thus, in Chapter 1 I discussed some of the seminal models of the Information Society, and in Chapter 2 I explored the digital divide metaphor. I argued that for both the models and the metaphor, far too much attention is placed on economic and technological changes. The flash mobs and flash robberies are not about changes in the economy and have nothing to do with technological advances. And so like most of the social accomplishments in the Information Society, they are not seen as anything truly significant. We are amused at the flash mobs, horrified by the flash robs. But our focus is still squarely on the latest IPO offering from a new tech company, or the number of tech jobs added to the American economy.

In Chapter 3 I introduced the concepts "digital environment" and "digital practices". The digital environment is defined as the social space produced through interconnected information and communication technologies (ICTs). The digital environment, or DE, is distinct from the physical environment, or PE. It is a space where one must enter into via ICTs. Upon entry, one is faced with a new set of social forces, the navigation of which requires adopting new behaviors. Digital practices, then, are the behaviors that result when groups navigate the digital environment. These digital practices do not arise at random, but are the consequences of historical patterns and the current structural conditions. People enter into the DE, and based upon what they already know and what they currently need, they leverage the properties of the DE accordingly. It is ultimately the uncovering of these new digital practices and exploring their consequences for the social structure of society that identifies a "digital practice perspective".

A digital practice perspective could supply the tools necessary to understand the rash of flash robberies. Undoubtedly, they were instances where the street corner culture of poor and working class inner-city settings (as opposed to the living room culture of suburban middle class settings) lent themselves to kids plotting deviance. The norm of young men roaming street corners meant that youth were already accustomed to traveling in these spaces in small groups. It made the synergy of communication and information sharing in the DE with fast physical action in the PE much easier. It is hard to imagine, again because it is so counterintuitive. But these youths were, on this measure, the "haves" in the DE. Meanwhile, the upper and middle class whites they attacked, and the business owners and law enforcement that they flummoxed, were the "have nots".

In Chapters 4, 5, and 6 I presented three studies that explore the digital practices of African Americans. In Chapter 4 I looked at the digital practice of building weak ties online. African Americans are more likely to make attempts at building connections with new people on social networking sites. This practice is based on a wealth of strong ties in the physical environment, but a dearth of weak ties. African Americans attempt to redress this imbalance in the PE on sites like Facebook and LinkedIn. In Chapter 5 I explored the more intensive use of the mobile phone by African Americans—the digital practice of maintaining family ties via mobile phone. The higher rates of mobile phone usage by African Americans can be explained in part by a complex family structure and the cultural precedent of maintaining ties with extended family members. In Chapter 6 I explored the digital practice of producing black only spaces for communication. Throughout their long history in the United States, African Americans have constructed spaces for communication in the PE that allow them an opportunity to construct and manage narratives about the world from a black perspective. This digital practice reasserts itself in the DE. Chapters 4, 5, and 6 were exhibits A, B, and C in my case for a digital practice perspective.

I chose African Americans because my African American background produced an inherent interest, and my knowledge of African American social and cultural conditions made it easier for me to apply the digital practice perspective to them. The fact is that minorities, and here I am mainly referring to African Americans and Hispanics, are not as disadvantaged vis-à-vis ICTs as one might think. Minorities have become very adept at using technology to overcome structural and historical difficulties, so much so that I cannot imagine labeling them disadvantaged with respect to this domain of life.

The digital practice perspective not only helps us identify important patterns of social interaction, it also helps us reinterpret phenomena. We can see the social significance in a given pattern. We can see that the new technologies produced are not the be all and end all of the discussion—who made it, who can sell it, and who can buy it. What also matters are the ways that groups at the ground level are appropriating these technologies and using them to achieve their goals. But making the Internet less free and less open will hinder groups' abilities to explore the DE and leverage its properties. And so in Chapter 7 I discuss some of the more important federal policies that can affect the free and open Internet. These policies are the Telecommunication Act of 1996, the Digital Millennium Copyright Act of 1998, the Federal Communication Commission Policy Statement: Preserving the Free and Open Internet in 2010, and The National Broadband Plan of 2010. Policy has been focused on making the digital environment amenable to commerce by increasing the number of businesses (producers) and increasing the number of users (consumers). This is potentially to the detriment of nonmarket spaces where the social, cultural, and civic potential of the digital environment is housed. The flash robs occurred because groups—even in the lowest socioeconomic strata—are able to play with the DE, and leverage it to meet their needs. We may not like the outcome of this *particular* tinkering with the DE, but it is in the tinkering that we see the potential.

In conclusion, the Information Society is an age of social and cultural transformation as well as technological and economic. The primary purpose of *The Digital Practices of African Americans: An Approach to Studying Cultural Change in the Information Society* is to construct a new lens through which to identify and understand these social and cultural transformations. Only when society's leaders—the academics, writers, activists, and politicians who mold public opinion and guide the public dialogue—begin to acknowledge the power inherent in the non-economic aspects of our Information Society can we truly harness the power of new technology. Social change will occur in the Information Society not through economic transformations or through faster and cheaper technology, but through everyday people figuring out the best way to manage their lives given the technology they have available. Social progress, social transformations, and social revolutions in the physical environment will only occur through the creation of digital practices in the digital environment.

Appendix

APPENDIX A

The range for making phone calls was 0 (minimum) to 500 (maximum). The mean was 13.10, with a standard deviation of 28.4. The range for making text messages was 0 (minimum) to 500 (maximum). The mean was 39.10, with a standard deviation of 89.9. The raw measures for number of phone calls and number of text messages are not amenable to a regression analysis as they do not follow normal distributions and exhibit high levels of skewness. These raw numbers were transformed into ordinal variables. Each variable was cut into eight units at cut points at the 5th, 10th, 25th, 50th, 75th, 90th, and 95th percentiles [see below]. After transformations, the mean for phone calls was 3.38, and the standard deviation was 1.70. The mean for text messages was 3.19, and the standard deviation was 1.72.

Transformations for Phone Calls and Text Messages

Phone Calls			Text Messages		
Percentile	Range	Value	Percentile	Range	Value
5	0	0	5	0	0
10	1	1	10	1	1
25	2-3	2	25	2	2
50	4-5	3	50	3-10	3
75	6-12	4	75	11-30	4
90	13-25	5	90	31-100	5
95	26-41	6	95	101-200	6
100	42 and over	7	100	Over 200	7

APPENDIX B

Total Variance Explained

	Initial Eigenvalues			Rotation Sums of Squared Loadings		
Component	Total	% of Variance	Cumulative %	Total	% of Variance	Cumulative %
1	4.148	37.709	37.709	2.796	25.418	25.418
2	1.386	12.596	50.304	1.774	16.124	41.542
3	1.181	10.735	61.040	1.702	15.477	57.018
4	1.063	9.663	70.702	1.505	13.684	70.702

Rotated Component Matrix[a]

	Component Number and Title			
	(1) "Text Chat"	(2) "Work"	(3) "Coordinate"	(4) "Voice Chat"
How often do you call just to say hello and chat?				.872
How often do you call to report where you are or check on where someone is?			.824	
How often do you call to coordinate where you are physically meeting someone?			.725	
How often do you call to do things related to work?		.881		
How often do you call to have a long conversation to discuss important things?				.677

Rotated Component Matrix[a]

	Component Number and Title			
	(1) "Text Chat"	(2) "Work"	(3) "Coordi-nate"	(4) "Voice Chat"
How often do you send or receive texts just to say hello and chat?	.719			
How often do you send or receive text messages to report where you are or check on where someone else is?	.660		.518	
How often do you send or receive text messages to coordinate where you are physically meeting someone?	.734			
How often do you send or receive text messages to do things related to work?		.821		
How often do you send or receive text messages to have a long exchange discussing important personal matters?	.766			
How often do you send or receive text messages to exchange information quietly when you can't make a voice call?	.708			

Extraction Method: Principal Component Analysis.
Rotation Method: Varimax with Kaiser Normalization.

APPENDIX C

	No. of Phone Calls (Raw)		No. of Text Messages (Raw)	
	Model 1 "Before Family"	Model 2 "After Family"	Model 1 "Before Family"	Model 2 "After Family"
Variables				
Controls				
Age	-.294***	-.283***	-.565***	-.532***
Female	-.073***	-.083***	.041**	.043***
Education (Comparison Variable is HS Diploma)				
- Less than HS	-.007	-.009	-.001	-.005
- Some College/Tech School	-.015	-.004	-.092***	-.088***
- Bachelor's Degree or More	-.038**	-.027	-.110***	-.096***
Family Income (Compared to Income between $30 and $75,000				
- Less than $10,000	-.026*	-.022	-.051***	-.049***
- Between $10 and $30,000	.044***	.046***	.044**	.045**
- More than $75,000	.082***	.075***	.063***	.072***
Employment (Compared to Employed Full Time)				
- Part Time	-.056***	-.056***	.076***	.061***
- Retired	-.105***	-.091***	.031*	.024
- Unemployed	-.077***	-.076***	.016	.005
Race (African Americans Compared to All Other Ethnoracial Groups)				
- African American	.141***	.143***	.068***	.061***
Family Type				
Marital Status (Comparison Variable is Married)				
- Cohabitating		.053***		.048***
- Divorced/Separated/Widowed		.033**		.051***
- Never Married or Single		-.020		.069***
Family Size				
- Number of Children in Home		.099***		.021
- Number of Adults in Home		.046***		.068***
Adjusted R^2	.166	.180	.352	.359

Regression Model Showing Betas for Phone Calls and Text Messages

APPENDIX D

	Text (Factor)		Work (Factor)	
Variables	Model 1 "Before Family"	Model 2 "After Family"	Model 1 "Before Family"	Model 2 "After Family"
Controls				
Age	-.414***	-.353***	.000	.031
Female	.026	.035**	-.267***	-.271***
Education (Comparison Variable is HS Diploma)				
- Less than HS	.046**	.037*	.040**	.044**
- Some College/Tech School	-.018	-.027	.047**	.059***
- Bachelor's Degree or More	.011	.017	.080***	.087***
Family Income (Compared to Income between $30 and $75,000				
- Less than $10,000	.013	.007	-.078***	-.077***
- Between $10 and $30,000	.053***	.057***	.030*	.039**
- More than $75,000	.007	.026	.113***	.115***
Employment (Compared to Employed Full Time)				
- Part Time	.116***	.094***	-.092***	-.096***
- Retired	.005	-.006	-.108***	-.104***
- Unemployed	.111***	.093***	-.219***	-.225***
Race (African Americans Compared to All Other Ethnoracial Groups)				
- African American	.055***	.039**	.056***	.049***
Family Type				
Marital Status (Comparison Variable is Married)				
- Cohabitating		.000		.061***
- Divorced/Separated/Widowed		.042**		-.003
- Never Married or Single		.142***		.052**
Family Size				
- Number of Children in Home		-.011		.101***
- Number of Adults in Home		.057***		-.006
Adjusted R²	.239	.258	.188	.198

Regression Model Showing Betas for "Text" and "Work" Activities

APPENDIX E

	Coordinate (Factor)		Chat (Factor)	
Variables	Model 1 "Before Family"	Model 2 "After Family"	Model 1 "Before Family"	Model 2 "After Family"
Controls				
Age	-.072***	-.063**	-.022	-.009
Female	.010	.007	.117***	.109***
Education (Comparison Variable is HS Diploma)				
- Less than HS	.023	.033*	.007	.009
- Some College/Tech School	.042*	.055**	-.021	-.003
- Bachelor's Degree or More	.073***	.081***	-.113***	-.101***
Family Income (Compared to Income Between $30 and $75,000				
- Less than $10,000	-.017	-.012	.023	.031*
- Between $10 and $30,000	.045**	.055**	.094***	.098***
- More than $75,000	.015	-.004	-.005	-.003
Employment (Compared to Employed Full Time)				
- Part Time	.041**	. 040*	-.041**	-.043**
- Retired	-.007	-.001	.023	.029
- Unemployed	-.022	-.022	-.077***	-.077***
Race (African Americans Compared to All Other Ethnoracial Groups)				
- African American	-.008	.000	.160***	.163***
Family Type				
Marital Status (Comparison Variable is Married)				
- Cohabitating		.012		.112***
- Divorced/Separated/Widowed		-.070***		-.005
- Never Married or Single		-.031		-.002
Family Size				
- Number of Children in Home		.075***		.088***
- Number of Adults in Home		.014		.028
Adjusted R²	.011	.021	.066	.084

Regression Model Showing Betas for "Coordinate" and "Chat" Activities

Notes

CHAPTER ONE: THE INFORMATION SOCIETY

1. Emblematic of this genre is the 2010 documentary *inside Job* (https://en.wikipedia.org/wiki/Inside_Job_(film)).
2. To be precise, Bell wrote that the industrial society was a game of man against *fabricated* nature, meaning that man worked with machines (see Bell 1973, p. 116).
3. Castells' use of the terms information age and network society can be a bit confusing. His entire trilogy is called *The Information Age: Economy, Society, and Culture*. However, throughout the trilogy he refers to modern times as the "network society". I am inclined to believe that when referring to all domains of society as an integrated whole—the cultural, political, and economic, "information age" is most fitting, and when talking about specific dynamics between corporations or between groups, "network society" is the most fitting.
4. In brief, world systems theory, popularized by Immanuel Wallerstein, posits that understanding the modern nation requires analyzing its position vis-à-vis other nations. All modern nations are enmeshed in a capitalist world system that operates by more powerful nations extracting surplus from less powerful ones. Nations can be organized into three categories. The most developed nations, the "core" nations, contain the largest and most profitable corporations, while the least developed nations, the "periphery" nations have few developed industries and mainly supply low cost labor and resources. World systems theory assumes a conflict relationship between nations. Rich nations are exploiting poor ones through this relationship, and they are only rich *because* of this exploitative relationship.

5. Part I of his book (pp. 35–132) lays out an understanding of information and cultural production in modern society. Of special interest is his chapter entitled "Some Basic Economics of Information Production and Innovation" (pp. 35–58). This is an indispensable chapter when one wishes to understand key differences between what is produced online as opposed to what is produced in the physical environment.

CHAPTER TWO: THE DIGITAL DIVIDE

1. Web 1.0 and Web 2.0 are terms used to describe different phases in the development of the Internet, especially as it pertains to website and the user experience. Web 1.0 describes an early version of the web where websites were mainly static billboards where users could read and download information. Web 2.0 represents the shift towards more interactive websites, where websites are tailored to the uniqueness of the user, and where the user can modify the website to her needs.
2. More specifically, the federal government, which had invested in the technology and the development of the Internet, opened up the Internet to commercial traffic. See (http://www.merit.edu/networkresearch/projecthistory/nsfnet/nsfnet_article.php).
3. If we think globally, however, this metaphor still retains its original meaning. People living in developing nations still do not have adequate access to computers and the Internet (although access to mobile phones is often readily available). The "one laptop per child" campaigns are attempts to bridge this gap.
4. See the ITU's annual report "Measuring the Information Society" (http://www.itu.int/ITU-D/ict/publications/idi/material/2011/MIS_2011_without_annex_5.pdf).
5. For some, the digital divide is a moral issue. In this case, one does not need evidence of consequences if one views the lack of Internet access as a human right.
6. See "Technology Trends among People of Color" (http://www.pewinternet.org/Commentary/2010/September/Technology-Trends-Among-People-of-Color.aspx).
7. This report can be found at: http://www.pewinternet.org/Media-Mentions/2011/For-minorities-new-digital-divide-seen.aspx.

CHAPTER THREE: THE DIGITAL PRACTICE PERSPECTIVE

1. A good application of this idea can be seen in political science. A debate is currently underway about the efficacy of "netroots" organizations such as MoveOn.org that use the low transaction costs of the web to enlist thousands of supporters for various causes. However, some scholars argue that the low transaction costs mean that there is little more than symbolism in the members who join these organizations or sign online petitions.
2. Organizations like businesses, non-profits, and governments can organize people to conduct an activity by paying people to work together to produce a product. Consider mining for oil. This activity cannot be done without an organization willing to buy the materials and provide wages for people to perform the tasks needed to mine for oil. The organization

is willing to give wages to workers because the oil extracted will net a profit over and above what was invested.

3. This phrase was initially used by Melvin Webber in his essay "Order in Diversity: Community without Propinquity" (1963). In this essay Webber argued that many subcultures were forming in urban environments, organized around lifestyle as opposed to neighborhood. Calhoun uses the phrase in conjunction with ICTs.

4. The use of the terms "wild" and "tame" are not an artistic license. These terms are used within domestication of technology studies. See Haddon (2011).

5. Massively Open Online Courses.

CHAPTER FOUR: THE DIGITAL PRACTICE OF WEAK TIE DEVELOPMENT

1. In general, individuals with more social capital are better off than those with less. However, social capital is not an unqualified good. Situations may arise where bonding and bridging capital is at odds with each other. Communities with high levels of bonding capital will reap benefits through increased trust of neighbors, more sharing of resources, and richer social interactions. However, these communities may become clannish, suspicious, and closed to outsiders, making it difficult for members to form bridges to new groups. Stack (1974) makes this point in *All Our Kin* when she notes that the strength of the black extended family often makes it difficult for outsiders to develop intimate connections with those family members. Putnam (2000) also makes this point using the school integration fights of the civil rights era: "Proponents of busing believed that only through racially integrated schools could America ever generate sufficient social capital—familiarity, tolerance, solidarity, trust, habits of co-operation, and mutual respect—across the racial divide. Opponents of busing replied that in most parts of America, neighborhood schools provided a unique site for building social capital—friendship, habits of cooperation, solidarity. The deepest tragedy of the busing controversy is that both sides were probably right." (362).

2. This phenomenon holds for all statuses and classes. Thus the wealthy are more likely to be friends with other wealthy people and Mormons are more likely to be friends with other Mormons. But race is the most salient predictor of who one is connected to (McPherson et al. 2001) and this is the truest for African Americans.

3. As opposed to the phrase "hooking up with someone", which has a decidedly different meaning!

4. Although other scholars have collaborated on some of the articles I reference, each study has at least two professors from the Michigan State University faculty: Charles Steinfield, Nicole Ellison, or Cliff Lampe.

5. We do not make specific claims about other ethnoracial groups. However, they were included in the analysis to add nuance and for comparison.

6. The Pew Internet and American Life Project conducts research that explores the impact of the Internet on individuals, families, communities, and on social, economic, political and religious institutions. The survey was conducted between April 8, 2008, and May 8, 2008, through telephone interviews of a random sample of adults age 18 or over. The survey asks

questions about respondents' Internet activities and attitudes towards technology. The response rate for this survey is 25%. The total number of respondents for this survey is 2251, with African American respondents numbering 215. Pew provides a weight for this survey derived from the Census Bureau's March 2007 Annual Social and Economic Supplement to correct for response bias.

7. An odds ratio greater than 1 for an independent variable indicates that the variable's effect is to increase the odds of "yes". Conversely, an odds ratio of less than 1 indicates that the variable's effect is to decrease the odds of "yes". Values above 1 represent percentage point increases, and values below 1 represent percentage point decreases. Similar to parameter estimates for ordinary least squares regression analysis, an odds ratio for nominal variables shows an increase in odds compared to the reference variable. For example, if in the model predicting the ownership of multiple social networking profiles we observe an odds ratio of .459 for income between $20,000 and $40,000, we can interpret this as: "The odds of owning profiles on multiple social networks for respondents with incomes between $20,000 and $40,000 is 54% less than for respondents with incomes between $40,000 and $100,000."

CHAPTER FIVE: THE DIGITAL PRACTICE OF MAINTAING TIES VIA MOBILE PHONE

1. "Mobile Access 2010" (Accessed April 4, 2013) http://www.pewinternet.org/Reports/2010/Mobile-Access-2010.aspx.
2. As I write this, the Korean electronics company Samsung has introduced the Galaxy Gear, a watch that also doubles as a phone. This makes it even easier to enter the digital environment in a variety of contexts.
3. An odds ratio greater than 1 for an independent variable indicates that the variable's effect is to increase the odds of "yes". Conversely, an odds ratio of less than 1 indicates that the variable's effect is to decrease the odds of "yes". Values above 1 represent percentage point increases, and values below 1 represent percentage point decreases. Similar to parameter estimates for ordinary least squares regression analysis, an odds ratio for nominal variables indicate an increase in odds compared to the reference variable.

CHAPTER SIX: THE DIGITAL PRACTICE OF MAINTAINING DIGITAL ENCLAVES

1. An interesting website that collects microaggressions as reported by the people themselves is "The Microaggressions Project" (http://www.microaggressions.com/).
2. In his iconic work *Souls of Black Folk*, Dubois writes: "Between me and the other world there is ever an unasked question: unasked by some through feelings of delicacy; by others through the difficulty of rightly framing it. All, nevertheless, flutter round it. They approach me in a half-hesitant sort of way, eye me curiously or compassionately, and then, instead of saying directly, How does it feel to be a problem?" (1).

3. This data was collected on 1/25/2013 from www.alexa.com. Traffic rank is "is based on three months of aggregated historical traffic data from millions of Alexa Toolbar users and data obtained from other, diverse traffic data sources, and is a combined measure of page views and users (reach). As a first step, Alexa computes the reach and number of page views for all sites on the web on a daily basis. The main Alexa traffic rank is based on a value derived from these two quantities averaged over time (so that the rank of a site reflects both the number of users who visit that site as well as the number of pages on the site viewed by those users). The three-month change is determined by comparing the site's current rank with its rank from three months ago. For example, on July 1, the three-month change would show the difference between the rank based on traffic during the first quarter of the year and the rank based on traffic during the second quarter" (Alexa.com).

4. For a discussion on the concentration of online traffic, see Ch. 5 of Hindman (2009).

5. The algorithm works by splitting a network into two mutually exclusive communities, such that the number of connections within a community is greater than by chance alone. For example, the initial 41 websites would be split into two communities of say, community A composed of 17 websites, and community B composed of 24 websites. The process is then repeated for the two newly formed communities. The algorithm continues until it reaches a predetermined splitting point. Like other types of splitting or partitioning processes such as factor analysis and classification trees, the researcher chooses where to stop the splitting process. The standard for factor analysis is an eigenvalue of 1, and I use the same standard here.

6. http://www.theroot.com/views/politics.

7. http://www.theroot.com/views/gops-three-fifths-compromise.

8. http://www.theroot.com/views/acting-white-theory-doesnt-add.

9. http://www.theroot.com/views/are-we-black-no-more-not-quite.

10. http://www.theroot.com/views/slaves-letter-reveals-pace-freedom.

11. http://www.theroot.com/views/are-we-black-no-more-not-quite.

12. http://www.theroot.com/views/new-cbc-leader-were-not-just-blacks.

13. http://www.theroot.com/views/are-we-black-no-more-not-quite.

14. http://www.theroot.com/views/our-kids-arent-treated-equally-school.

CHAPTER SEVEN: THE DIGITAL PRACTICE PERSPECTIVE AND SOCIAL POLICY: IMPROVING THE SOCIAL, CULTURAL, AND CIVIC QUALITY OF THE DIGITAL ENVIRONMENT

1. A good summary of the Telecommunications ACT of 1996 can be found at "The Telecommunication Act of 1996: an Overview", by L. Fredrik Cederqvist (http://merlin.obs.coe.int/iris/1996/3/article9.en.html).

2. Technically, the FCC classifies incumbents as ILECs (Incumbent Local Exchange Carriers) and competitors as CLECs (Competing Local Exchange Carriers).

3. See http://hraunfoss.fcc.gov/edocs_public/attachmatch/DOC-318397A1.pdf.

4. A summary of these programs can be found at http://transition.fcc.gov/wcb/tapd/universal_service/.

5. At the time of this writing, the current Librarian of Congress is James H. Billington.
6. http://www.timwu.org/network_neutrality.html, Accessed April 27, 2013.
7. The policy statement can be found at http://hraunfoss.fcc.gov/edocs_public/attachmatch/ FCC-10-201A1_Rcd.pdf, Accessed May 3, 2013.
8. The text of the plan can be found at www.broadband.gov/plan, accessed May 4, 2013. For a good summary of the major elements of the plan see: Jim Carney, Michael Celli, Cate Cravath, Delara Derakhshani, Michael Rooney, Matthew Starr, and Preston Thomas (2010). "Conspectus: Overview of the National Broadband Plan". CommLaw Conspectus 517. (2010): 16141 words. LexisNexis Academic. Web. Date Accessed: March 5, 2013.
9. This is megabits per second. As a point of comparison, my home Internet connection at the time of this writing is 54Mbps, which is close to the median speed for cable Internet service.
10. http://www.alexa.com/topsites.
11. http://en.wikipedia.org/wiki/Digerati.
12. This idea comes from a notable paper published in *The Journal of Behavioral and Brain Sciences*. See Joseph Henrich, Steven J. Heine and Ara Norenzayan (2010). Behavioral and Brain Sciences, 33 (2-3): 61–83. Since its initial publication it has appeared in numerous other publications. The authors argue that much of psychological research is based on white undergraduate students from wealthy families, but these students are outliers in their value orientations and cultural attitudes.
13. The Web Use Project can be found at http://www.webuse.org/index.html, Accessed May 12, 2013.
14. The FCC has conducted several studies as recommended by the National Broadband Plan (see survey here: http://hraunfoss.fcc.gov/edocs_public/attachmatch/DOC-296444A1. pdf). Also, the Pew Internet and American Life Project, from which a good deal of the data in this book comes, administers surveys.

CHAPTER EIGHT: CONCLUSION: SMART MOBS, FLASH MOBS, FLASH ROBS AND THE REVOLUTIONARY POTENTIAL OF THE DIGITAL ENVIRONMENT

1. Wasik has made the correspondence of his e-mails available at his website: http://billwasik. com/post/104403795/the-mob-project. All e-mails about Wasik come from this website.
2. http://abcnews.go.com/WNT/video/flash-mobs-robbing-stores-20834910.

References

Ahrens, Frank. 2008. "Post Launches Site with African American Focus." *The Washington Post*, January 28. Retrieved January 25, 2012 (http://www.washingtonpost.com/wp-dyn/content/article/2008/01/27/AR2008012701672.html).

Alba, Richard, John R. Logan, and Brian J. Stults. 2000. "How Segregated Are Middle Class Americans?" *Social Problems* 47(4): 543–558.

Attewell, Paul. 2001. "The First and Second Digital Divides." *Sociology of Education* 74(3): 252–259.

Baker, Jonathan, Mark Bykowsky, Patrick DeGraba, Paul LaFontaine, Eric Ralph, and William Sharkey. 2011. "The Year in Economics at the FCC, 2010–11: Protecting Competition Online." *Review of Industrial Organization* 39(4): 297–309.

Barnett, Marina. 2004. "A Qualitative Analysis of Family Support and Interaction among Black College Students at an Ivy League University." *Journal of Negro Education* 73(1): 53–68.

Baron, Robert and Norbert Kerr. 2002. *Group Process, Group Decision, Group Action, 2nd ed.* Philadelphia, PA: Open University Press.

Baym, Nancy. 2010. *Personal Connections in the Digital Age*. Malden, MA: Polity Press.

Behtoui, Alireza and Anders Neergard. 2010. "Social Capital and Wage Disadvantages among Immigrant Workers." *Work, Employment, and Society* 24(4): 761–779.

Bell, Daniel. 1973. *The Coming of Post-Industrial Society: A Venture in Social Forecasting*. New York, NY: Basic Books.

Benkler, Yochai. 2007. *The Wealth of Networks: How Social Production Transforms Markets and Freedom*. New Haven, CT: Yale University Press.

Bertrand, Marianne and Sendhil Mullaninathan. 2004. "Are Emily and Greg More Employable than Lakisha and Jamal? A Field Experiment of Labor Market Discrimination." *The American Economic Review* 94(4): 991–1013.

Bonilla-Silva, Eduardo. 1997. "Rethinking Racism: Toward a Structural Interpretation." *American Sociological Review* 62(3): 465–480.

Bourdieu, Pierre. 1984. *Distinction: A Social Critique of the Judgment of Taste.* Cambridge, MA: Harvard University Press.

Bourdieu, Pierre. 1985. "The Forms of Capital." Pp. 241–258 in *Handbook of Theory and Research for the Sociology of Education,* edited by J. G. Richardson. New York, NY: Greenwood Press.

Boyd, Danah. 2011. "White Flight in Networked Publics: How Race and Class Shaped American Teen Engagement with MySpace and Facebook." Pp. 146–167 in *Race After the Internet,* Lisa Nakamura and Peter Chow-White. *Race after the Internet.* New York, NY: Routledge. 146–167.

Boyd, Danah and Nicole Ellison. 2007. "Social Network Sites: Definition, History, and Scholarship." *Journal of Computer-Mediated Communication* 13 (1): 210–230.

Brinkerhoff, Jennifer M. 2009. *Digital Diasporas: Identity and Transnational Engagement.* Cambridge: Cambridge University Press.

Brooks, Joanna. 2005. "The Early American Public Sphere and the Emergence of a Black Print Counterpublic." *The William and Mary Quarterly,* 62(1): 67–92.

Burt, Ronald S. 1995. *Structural Holes: The Social Structure of Competition.* Cambridge, MA: Harvard University Press.

Byrne, Dara. N. 2007. "Public Discourse, Community Concerns, and Civic Engagement: Exploring Black Social Networking Traditions on BlackPlanet.com." *Journal of Computer-Mediated Communication,* 13(1). Retrieved August 11, 2011 (http://jcmc.indiana.edu/vol13/issue1/byrne.html).

Calhoun, Craig. 1998. "Community without Propinquity Revisited: Communications Technology and the Transformation of the Urban Public Sphere." *Sociological Inquiry* 68(3): 373–397.

Cantor, Marjorie, Mark Brennan, and Anthony Sainz. 1994. "The Importance of Ethnicity in the Social Support Systems of Older New Yorkers: A Longitudinal Perspective (1970–1990)." *Journal of Gerontological Social Work* 22(3–4): 95–128.

Carney, Jim, Michael Celli, Cate Cravath, Delara Derakhshani, Michael Rooney, Matthew Starr, and Preston Thomas. 2010. "Conspectus: Overview of the National Broadband Plan." *18 CommLaw Conspectus 517.* (Retrieved from LexisNexis Academic on May 3, 2013).

Castells, Manuel. 2000a. *The Rise of the Network Society, The Information Age: Economy, Society and Culture Vol. I, 2nd ed.* Malden, MA: Blackwell Publishers.

———. 2004. *The Power of Identity, The Information Age: Economy, Society and Culture Vol. II, 2nd ed.* Malden, MA: Blackwell Publishers.

———. 2000b. *End of Millennium, The Information Age: Economy, Society and Culture Vol. III.* Malden, MA: Blackwell Publishers.

Cavanagh, Allison. 2007. *Sociology in the Age of the Internet.* New York, NY: Open University Press.

Census.gov. 2010a. "Income, Poverty, and Health Insurance Coverage in the United States: 2009." Retrieved February 3, 2012 (http://www.census.gov/prod/2010pubs/p60-238.pdf).

Census.gov 2010b. "Households and Families: 2010." Retrieved March 29, 2012 (http://www.census.gov/prod/cen2010/briefs/c2010br-14.pdf).

Cohen, Julie. 2012. *Configuring the Networked Self: Law, Code, and the Play of Everyday Practice.* New Haven, CT: Yale University Press.

Coleman, James. 1988. "Social Capital in the Creation of Human Capital." *American Journal of Sociology* 94: S95–S120.

Conley, Dalton. 1999. *Being Black: Living in the Red: Race, Wealth, and Social Policy in America.* Berkeley, CA: University of California Press.

Crang, Michael, Tracey Crosbie, and Stephen Graham. 2006. "Variable Geometries of Connection: Urban Digital Divides and the Uses of Information Technology." *Urban Studies,* 43(13): 2551–2570.

Curran, James. 2012. "Rethinking Internet History." Pp. 34–76 in *Misunderstanding the Internet,* edited by J. Curran, N. Fenton, and D. Freedman. New York, NY: Routledge.

Daniels, Jesse. 2009. *Cyberracism: White Supremacy Online and the New Attack on Civil Rights.* New York, NY: Rowman and Littlefield.

Dawson, Michael. 1995. "A Black Counterpublic?: Economic Earthquakes, Racial Agenda(s), and Black Politics." Pp. 199–228 in *The Black Public Sphere: A Public Culture Book,* edited by The Black Public Sphere Collective. Chicago, IL: University of Chicago Press.

———. 2001. *Black Visions: The Roots of Contemporary African–American Political Ideologies.* Chicago, Il: The University of Chicago Press.

DiMaggio, P., Eszter Hargittai, Coral Celeste and Steven Shafer. 2004. "Digital Inequality: From Unequal Access to Differentiated Use." Pp. 355–400 in *Social Inequality,* edited by K. Nekerman. New York, NY: Russell Sage Foundation.

Donner, Jonathan. 2007. "The Rules of Beeping: Exchanging Messages via Intentional 'Missed Calls' on Mobile Phones" *Journal of Computer-Mediated Communication,* 13 (1). Retrieved February 15, 2012 (http://jcmc.indiana.edu/vol13/issue1/donner.html).

Drotner, Kirsten. 2005. "Media on the Move: Personalized Media and the Transformation of Publicness." *Journal of Media Practice* 6(1): 53–64.

DuBois, W.E.B. 1903 [1994]. *The Souls of Black Folk.* Mineola, NY: Dover Publications.

Dugan, Robert E. and Jennifer L. Souza. 1996. "Cycles, a Crystal Ball, and the Telecommunications Act of 1996—Been There, Done That." *Journal of Academic Librarianship* 22(6): 457–462.

Durkheim, Emile. 1895. *The Rules of Sociological Method.* New York, NY: The Free Press.

Elliott, James R. 1999. "Social Isolation and Labor Market Insulation: Network and Neighborhood Effects on Less-Educated Urban Workers." *The Sociological Quarterly* 40 (2): 199–216.

Ellison, Nicole, Charles Steinfield, and Cliff Lampe. 2007. "The Benefits of Facebook 'Friends': Social Capital and College Students' Use of Online Social Network Sites." *Journal of Computer-Mediated Communication* 12(4): 1143–1168.

Ellison, Nicole B., Charles Steinfield, and Cliff Lampe. 2011. "Connection Strategies: Social Capital Implications of Facebook-Enabled Communication Practices." *New Media and Society* 13(6): 873–892.

Erickson, Bonnie H. 2004. "The Distribution of Gendered Social Capital in Canada." Pp. 27–50 in *The Creation and Returns of Social Capital*, edited by H. Flap and B. Volker. London: Routledge.

Everett, Anna. 2009. *Digital Diaspora: A Race for Cyberspace*. Albany, NY: State University of New York Press.

Facebook. 2012. "Statistics." Retrieved January 8, 2012 (http://www.facebook.com/press/info.php?statistics).

Feagin, Joe. 2000. *Racist America: Roots, Current Realities, and Future Reparations*. New York, NY: Routledge.

Federal Communications Commission. 2012. "Connecting America." Retrieved May 23, 2013 (http://www.fcc.gov/encyclopedia/connecting-america).

Flanagan, William. 2010. *Urban Sociology: Images and Structure*. Lanham, MD: Rowman and Littlefield.

Fraser, Nancy. 1990. "Rethinking the Public Sphere: A Contribution to the Critique of Actually Existing Democracy." *Social Text* 25/26: 56–90.

Freeman, Linton. 1978. "Centrality in Social Networks Conceptual Clarification," *Social Networks* 1: 215–239.

Fruchterman, Thomas M. and Edward Reingold. 1991. "Graph Drawing by Force-Directed Placement." *Software – Practice and Experience* 21(11):1129–1164.

Gertner, Jon. 2003. "The 3rd Annual Year in Ideas." *New York Times*, December 14. Retrieved June 10, 2013 (http://www.nytimes.com/2003/12/14/magazine/2003-the-3rd-annual-year-in-ideas-social-networks.html).

Giddens, Anthony. 1986. *The Constitution of Society: Outline of the Theory of Structuration*. Berkeley, CA: University of California Press.

Glanville, Jennifer L. and Jayne Beinenstock. 2009. "A Typology for Understanding the Connections among Different Forms of Social Capital." *American Behavioral Scientist* 52(11): 1507–1530.

Goldsmith, Jack and Timothy Wu. 2006. *Who Controls the Internet: Illusion of a Borderless World*. Oxford: Oxford University Press.

Gotved, Stine. 2002. "Spatial Dimensions in Online Communities." *Space and Culture* 5(4): 405–414.

Gowan, Teresa. 2011. "What's Social Capital Got to Do with It? The Ambiguous (and Overstated) Relationship between Social Capital and Ghetto Underemployment." *Critical Sociology* 37(1): 47–66.

Graham, Roderick. 2010. "ICT as Cultural Practice: Group Differences in Attitudes towards Technology among Americans" *New Media and Society* 12(6): 985–1003.

———. 2012. "The Digital Practice of Mobile Phones" *Sociology Compass* 12(6): 962–973.

Granovetter, Mark S. 1973. "The Strength of Weak Ties." *The American Journal of Sociology* 78(6): 1360–1380.

Grogger, Jeffrey. 2011. "Speech Patterns in Racial Wage Inequality." *Journal of Human Resources* 46(1): 1–25.

Habermas, Jurgen. (1989 [1962]) *The Structural Transformation of the Public Sphere: An Inquiry into a Category of Bourgeois Society*. Cambridge: Polity Press.

Haddon, Leslie. 2011. "Domestication Analysis, Objects of Study, and the Centrality of Technologies in Everyday Life." *Canadian Journal of Communication* 36(2): 311–323.

Hafner, Katie and Matthew Lyon. 1996. *Where Wizards Stay Up Late: The Origins of the Internet*. New York, NY: Simon and Schuster.

Hampton, Keith and Barry Wellman. 2003. "Neighboring in Netville: How the Internet Supports Community and Social Capital in a Wired Suburb." *City and Community* 2(4): 277–311.

Hargittai, Eszter. 2010. "Digital Na(t)ives? Variation in Internet Skills and Uses among Members of the 'Net Generation'." *Sociological Inquiry* 80(1): 92–113.

Hargittai, Eszter and Amanda Hinnant. 2008. "Digital Inequality: Differences in Young Adults' Use of the Internet." *Communication Research* 35(5): 602–621.

Hargittai, Eszter and Eden Litt. 2011. "The Tweet Smell of Celebrity Success: Explaining Variation in Twitter Adoption among a Diverse Group of Young Adults." *New Media and Society* 13(5): 824–842.

Harris-Lacewell, Melissa V. 2004. *Barbershops, Bibles, and BET: Everyday Talk and Black Political Thought*. Princeton, NJ: Princeton University Press.

Harvey, Adia M. 2005. "Becoming Entrepreneurs and the Helping Ideology: Intersection of Race, Gender, Class at the Black Beauty Salon." *Gender and Society* 19(6): 789–808.

Hassan, Robert. 2010. *The Information Society: Digital Media and Society Series*. Malden, MA: Polity Press.

Hays, Sharon. 1996. *The Cultural Contradictions of Motherhood*. New Haven, CT: Yale University Press.

Haythornthwaite, Carol. 2005. "Social Networks and Internet Connectivity Effects." *Information, Communication and Society* 8(2): 125–147.

Hill, Robert B. 1999. *The Strengths of Black Families: Twenty-five Years Later*. Lanham, MD: University Press of America.

Hindman, Matthew. 2009. *The Myth of Digital Democracy*. Princeton, NJ: Princeton University.

Horst, Heather and Daniel Miller. 2006. *The Cell Phone: An Anthropology of Communication*. New York, NY: Berg Publishers.

Hutchby, Ian. 2001. "Technologies, Texts and Affordances." *Sociology* 35(2): 441–456.

Ibarra, Herminia. 1995. "Race, Opportunity, and Diversity of Social Circles in Managerial Networks." *Academy of Management Journal* 38(3): 673–703.

Johnson, Colleen. 2004. "Perspectives on American Kinship in the Later 1990s." *Journal of Marriage and Family* 62(3): 623–639.

Johnson, Colleen L. and Barbara M. Barer. 1990. "Families and Networks among Older Inner-city Blacks." *The Gerontologist* 30 (6): 726–733.

Kadushin, Charles. 2012. *Understanding Social Networks: Theories, Concepts, and Findings*. Oxford: Oxford University Press.

Kakihara, Masao & Carsten Sørensen. 2002. Mobility: An Extended Perspective. *In Thirty-Fifth Hawaii International Conference on System Sciences* (HICSS-35), Big Island Hawaii, ed. R. S. Jr. IEEE.

Kang, Cecilia. 2010. "Support for Broadband Loses Speed; Blacks Gain More Access Older Americans Question Benefit." *Washington Post,* August 12. Retrieved October 11, 2012 (http://www.washingtonpost.com/wp-dyn/content/article/2010/08/11/AR2010081106216.html).

Katz, James E. and Mark A. Aakhus. 2002. *Perpetual Contact: Mobile Communication, Private Talk, Public Performance.* Cambridge: Cambridge University Press.

Kennedy, Tracy and Barry Wellman. 2007. "The Networked Household." *Information, Communication & Society* 10(5): 644–669.

Kimball, Danny. 2013. "What We Talk about When We Talk about Net Neutrality: A Historical Genealogy of the Discourse of 'Net Neutrality'." Pp. 33–48 in *Regulating the Web: Network Neutrality and the Fate of the Open Internet,* edited by Z. Stiegler. Lanham. MD: Lexington Books.

King, Jamilah. 2011. "How Big Telecom Used Smartphones to Create a New Digital Divide." Colorlines. Retrieved December 1, 2012 (http://colorlines.com/archives/2011/12/the_new_digital_divide_two_separate_but_unequal_internets.html).

Kvasny, Lynette and C. Frank Igwe. 2008. "An African American Weblog Community's Reading of AIDS in Black America." *Journal of Computer Mediated Communication* 13(3): 569–592.

Lareau, Annette. 2003. *Unequal Childhoods: Class, Race, and Family Life.* Berkeley, CA: University of California Press.

Lassen, David S. and Adam R. Brown. 2011. "Twitter: The Electoral Connection." *Social Science Computer Review* 29(4): 419–436.

Levy, Steven. 2010. *Hackers: Heroes of the Computer Revolution – 25ᵗʰ Anniversary Edition.* Sebastopol, CA: O'Reilly Media.

Ling, Rich. (2008a). *New Tech, New Ties: How Mobile Communication Is Reshaping Social Cohesion.* Cambridge, MA: MIT Press.

———. (2008b). "The Mediation of Ritual Interaction via the Mobile Telephone." Pp. 165–176 in *Handbook of Mobile Communication Studies,* edited by J. Katz. Cambridge, MA: MIT Press.

Ling, Rich, Troels Fibæk Bertel, and Pål Roe Sundsøy. 2012. "The Socio-demographics of Texting: An Analysis of Traffic Data." *New Media & Society* 14(2): 281–298.

Lohr, Steve. 1996. "A Nation Ponders Its Growing Digital Divide." *The New York Times,* October 21. Retrieved February 14 (http://www.nytimes.com/1996/10/21/business/a-nation-ponders-its-growing-digital-divide.html).

Loury, Glenn C. 1977. "A Dynamic Theory of Racial Income Differences." Pp. 153–186 in *Women, Minorities, and Employment Discrimination,* edited by P. A. Wallace and A. M. Lamond. Lexington, MA: Heath.

Lynn, Samara. 2012. "Guiding Women across the Digital Divide." *PCMag,* February 14. Retrieved February 19, 2012 (http://www.pcmag.com/article2/0,2817,2400243,00.asp).

Mackinnon, Rebecca. 2012. *Consent of the Networked: The Worldwide Struggle for Internet Freedom.* New York, NY: Basic Books.

Marketwire. 2011. "Social Job Seekers Getting Ahead: Jobvite Survey Reveals One in Six Workers Successfully Used Social Networks to Get Hired." Retrieved January 12, 2012 (http://www.marketwire.com/press-release/Social-Job-Seekers-Getting-Ahead-Jobvite-Survey-Reveals-One-Six-Workers-Successfully-1587676.htm).

Massey, Douglas and Garvey Lundey. 2001. "Use of Black English and Racial Discrimination in Urban Housing Markets New Methods and Findings." *Urban Affairs Review* 36(4): 452–469.

Mayer, Adalbert and Steven L. Puller. 2008. "The Old Boy (and Girl) Network: Social Network Formation on University Campuses." *Journal of Public Economics* 92(1–2): 329–347.

McCreary, Linda L. and Barbara L. Dancy. 2004. "Dimensions of Family Functioning: Perspectives of Low-Income African American Single-Parent Families." *Journal of Marriage and Family* 66 (3): 690–701.

McPherson, Miller, Lynn Smith-Lovin, and James M. Cook. 2001. "Birds of a Feather: Homophily in Social Networks." *Annual Review of Sociology* 27: 415–44.

Mehra, Bharat, Cecelia Merkel, and Ann Peterson Bishop. 2004. "The Internet for Empowerment of Minority and Marginalized Users." *New Media and Society* 6(6): 781–802.

Montlake, Simon. 2006. "China's Newest Shopping Craze: Team Buying." *Christian Science Monitor,* May 11. Retrieved November 11, 2012 (http://www.csmonitor.com/2006/0511/p01s01-woap.html).

Moren-Cross, Jennifer and Nan Lin. 2008. "Access to Social Capital and Status Attainment in the United States: Racial/Ethnic and Gender Differences." Pp. 364–379 in *Social Capital: An International Research Program,* edited by N. Lin and B. Erickson. Oxford: Oxford University Press.

Mossberger, Karen, Caroline J. Tolbert, and Mary Stansbury. 2003. *Virtual Inequality: Beyond the Digital Divide.* Washington, DC: Georgetown University Press.

Moynihan, Daniel P. 1965. *The Negro Family: A Case for National Action.* Washington, DC: Government Printing Office.

Nakamura, Lisa. 2002. *Cybertypes: Race, Ethnicity, and Identity on the Internet.* New York: Routledge.

———. 2008. *Digitizing Race: Visual Cultures on the Internet.* Minneapolis, MN: University of Minnesota Press.

Nakamura, Lisa, Peter Chow-White, and Alondra Nelson. 2011. *Race after the Internet.* New York, NY: Routledge.

National Archives – Clinton Presidential Material Project. 1996. "State of the Union Address." Retrieved December 1, 2012 (http://clinton6.nara.gov/1996/01/1996-01-23-president-state-of-the-union-address-as-delivered.html).

National Telecommunications and Information Administration. 1995. "Falling through the Net: A Survey of the 'Have Nots' in Rural and Urban America." Retrieved February 22, 2012 (http://www.ntia.doc.gov/ntiahome/fallingthru.html).

National Telecommunications and Information Administration. 1999. "Falling through the Net: Defining the Digital Divide." Retrieved February 23, 2012 (http://www.ntia.doc.gov/re port/1999/falling-through-net-defining-digital-divide).

Newman, Katherine. 1999. *No Shame in My Game: The Working Poor in the Inner City.* New York, NY: Knopf and Russell Sage.

Newman, Mark E. J. 2006. "Modularity and Community Structure in Networks." *Proceedings of the National Academy of Sciences of the United States of America* 103(23): 8577–8582.

Nie, Norman H. 2001. "Sociability, Interpersonal Relations, and the Internet: Reconciling Conflicting Findings." *American Behavioral Scientist* 45(3): 420–35.

Noble, Andrea. 2011. "County Proposes Flash-Mob Legislation; 7-Eleven Robbery Spurs Montgomery." *The Washington Times,* August 29th. Retrieved June 22, 2013 (http://www.wash ingtontimes.com/news/2011/aug/28/montgomery-county-proposes-flash-mob-law/).

Nuechterlein, Jonathan E. and Philip J. Weiser. 2005. *Digital Crossroads: American Telecommunications Policy in the Internet Age.* Cambridge, MA: The MIT Press.

Nunley, Vorris L. 2011. *Keepin' It Hushed: The Barbershop and African American Hush Harbor Rhetoric.* Detroit, MI: Wayne University Press.

Palfrey, John and Urs Gasser. 2008. *Born Digital: Understanding the First Generation of Digital Natives.* New York, NY: Basic Books.

Pariser, Eli. 2011. *The Filter Bubble: What the Internet Is Hiding from You.* New York, NY: Penguin Publishers.

Parks-Yancy, Rochelle, Nancy DiTomaso, and Corinne Post. 2009. "How Does Tie Strength Affect Access to Social Capital Resources for the Careers of Working and Middle Class African-Americans?" *Critical Sociology* 35(4): 541–563.

Petersen, Trond, Ishak Saporta, and Marc-David L. Seidel. 2000. "Offering a Job: Meritocracy and Social Networks." *American Journal of Sociology* 106(3): 763–816.

Peterson, Richard. A. and Robert M. Kern. 1996. "Changing Highbrow Taste: From Snob to Omnivore." *American Sociological Review* 61: 900–907.

Pew Internet and American Life. 2008. "Spring Tracking Survey." Retrieved January 27, 2011 (http://www.pewinternet.org/Reports/2008/Podcast-Downloading-2008/Ques tions-and-Data/Spring-Tracking-Survey-2008.aspx).

Portes, Alejandro. 1998. "Social Capital: Its Origins and Applications in Modern Sociology." *Annual Review of Sociology* 24: 1–24.

Putnam, Robert D. 2000. *Bowling Alone: The Collapse and Revival of American Community.* New York, NY: Simon and Schuster.

Rainie, Lee and Barry Wellman. 2012. *Networked: The New Social Operating System.* Cambridge, MA: MIT Press.

Rankin, Bruce and James M. Quane. 2000. "Neighborhood Poverty and the Social Isolation of Inner-City African-American Families." *Social Forces* 79(1): 139–164.

Rheingold, Howard. 1993. *The Virtual Community: Homesteading on the Electronic Frontier.* Cambridge, MA: MIT Press.

Rheingold, Howard. 2007. *Smart Mobs: The Next Digital Revolution.* New York, NY: Basic Books.

Rothenberg, Paula. 2011. *White Privilege*. New York, NY: Worth Publishers.

Sarkisian, Natalia. 2007. "Street Men, Family Men: Race and Men's Extended Family Involvement." *Social Forces* 86(2): 763–794.

Sarkisian, Natalia and Naomi Gerstel. 2004. "Kin Support among Blacks and Whites: Race and Family Organization." *American Sociological Review* 69(6): 812–837.

Schiller, Kurt. 2010. "A Simple Plan: Broadband and the FCC." *Information Today* 27(7):1–43.

Scott, James C. 1990. *Domination and the Arts of Resistance: Hidden Transcripts*. New Haven, CT: Yale University Press.

Shapiro, Thomas. 2005. *The Hidden Cost of Being African American: How Wealth Perpetuates Inequality*. New York, NY: Oxford University Press.

Shirky, Clay. 2008. *Here Comes Everybody: The Power of Organizing without Organizations*. New York, NY: Penguin.

Smith, Aaron. 2010. "Mobile Access 2010." Pew Internet and American Life Project. Retrieved December 1, 2010 (http://www.pewinternet.org/Reports/2010/Mobile-Access-2010.aspx).

Smith, Susan S. 2005. "'Don't Put My Name on It': Social Capital Activation and Job Finding Assistance among the Black Urban Poor." *American Journal of Sociology* 111(1): 1–57.

Sohn, Dongyoung and John D. Leckenby. 2007. "A Structural Solution to Communication Dilemmas in a Virtual Community." *Journal of Communication* 57(3): 435–449.

Stack, Carol. 1974. *All Our Kin*. New York, NY: Basic Books.

Stanley, Christine A. 2006. "Coloring the Academic Landscape: Faculty of Color Breaking the Silence in Predominantly White Colleges and Universities." *American Educational Research Journal* 43(4): 701–36.

Steinfield, Charles, Nicole Ellison, and Cliff Lampe. 2008. "Social Capital, Self-Esteem, and the Use of Online Social Network Sites: A Longitudinal Analysis." *Journal of Applied Developmental Psychology* 29(6): 434–445.

Steinfield, Charles, Joan M. DiMicco, Nicole B. Ellison, and Cliff Lampe. 2009. "Bowling Online: Social Networking and Social Capital within the Organization." *In Proceedings of the Fourth International Conference on Communities and Technologies* New York, NY, 245–254.

Stern, Micheal J. and Alison E. Adams. 2010. "Do Rural Residents Really Use the Internet to Build Social Capital? An Empirical Investigation." *American Behavioral Scientist* 53(9): 1389–1422.

Suber, Peter. 2012. *Open Access*. Cambridge, MA: MIT Press.

Subrahmanyam, Kaveri, Stephanie M. Reich, Natalia Waechter, and Guadalupe Espinoza. 2008. "Online and Offline Social Networks: Use of Social Networking Sites by Emerging Adults." *Journal of Applied Developmental Psychology* 29(6): 420–433.

Sunstein, Cass. 2001. *Republic.com*. Princeton, NJ: Princeton University Press.

———. 2007. *Republic.com 2.0*. Princeton, NJ: Princeton University Press.

Swidler, Ann. 1986. "Culture in Action: Symbols and Strategies." *American Sociological Review* 51(2): 273–286.

Tapscott, Don and Anthony D. Williams. (2010) *Wikinomics: How Mass Collaboration Changes Everything*. New York, NY: Portfolio.

Taylor, Robert J., Linda M. Chatters, and James S. Jackson. 1997. "Changes over Time in Support Network Involvement among African Americans." Pp. 295–318 in *Family Life in Black America*, edited by R.L. Taylor, J.S. Jackson, and L.M. Chatters. Thousand Oaks, CA:Sage.

Tigges, Leann M., Irene Browne, and Gary P. Green. 1998. "Social Isolation of the Urban Poor: Race, Class, and Neighborhood Effects on Social Resources." *Sociological Quarterly* 39(1): 53–77.

Tolnay, Stewart E. 1997. "The Great Migration and Changes in the Northern Black Family, 1940 to 1990." *Social Forces* 75(4): 1213–1238.

———. 2003. "The African American 'Great Migration' and Beyond." *Annual Review of Sociology* (29): 209–232.

Tolnay, Stewart E., Katherine J. Curtis White, Kyle D. Crowder, and Robert M. Adelman. 2005. "Distances Traveled during the Great Migration." *Social Science History* (29)4: 523–548.

Tomaskovic-Devey, Donald, Melvin Thomas, Kecia Johnson. 2005. "Race and the Accumulation of Human Capital across the Career: A Theoretical Model and Fixed-effects Application." *The American Journal of Sociology* 111(1): 58–89.

Turkle, Sherry. 2008. "Always-On/Always-On-You: The Tethered Self." Pp. 121–138 in *Handbook of Mobile Communication Studies*, edited by J. E. Katz. Cambridge, MA: MIT Press.

———. 1996. "Virtuality and Its Discontents, Searching for Community in Cyberspace," *The American Prospect* 7, no. 24.

———. 2011. *Alone Together: Why We Expect More from Technology and Less from Each Other*. New York, NY: Basic Books.

Van Dijk, Jan A.G.M. 2005. *The Deepening Divide: Inequality in the Information Society*. Thousand Oaks, CA: Sage.

Warschauer, Mark. 2003. *Technology and Social Inclusion: Rethinking the Digital Divide*. Cambridge, MA: MIT Press.

Webster, Frank. 2006. *Theories of the Information Society, 3rd ed.* New York, NY: Routledge.

Williams, Dmitri. 2006. "On and Off the 'net: Scales for Social Capital in an Online Era." *Journal of Computer-Mediated Communication* 11(2): 593–628.

Wilson, William J. 1978. *The Declining Significance of Race: Blacks and Changing American Institutions*. Chicago, IL: University of Chicago Press.

———. 1987. *The Truly Disadvantaged: The Inner City, the Underclass, and Public Policy*. Chicago, IlL: University of Chicago Press.

———. 2010. *More Than Just Race: Being Black and Poor in the Inner City*. New York, NY: Norton.

Wright, Erik O. 1994. *Interrogating Inequality: Essays on Class Analysis, Socialism and Marxism*. New York, NY: Verso.

Wu, Tim. 2003. "Network Neutrality, Broadband Discrimination." *Journal on Telecommunications and High Technology Law* 2(141–179).

Yang, Ke. 2008. "A Preliminary Study on the Use of Mobile Phones amongst Migrant Workers in Beijing" *Knowledge, Technology & Policy* 21(2), pp. 65–72.

Zittrain, Johnathan. 2008. *The Future of the Internet: And How to Stop It*. New Haven, CT: Yale University Press.

Index

Digital Formations

General Editor: *Steve Jones*

Digital Formations is the best source for critical, well-written books about digital technologies and modern life. Books in the series break new ground by emphasizing multiple methodological and theoretical approaches to deeply probe the formation and reformation of lived experience as it is refracted through digital interaction. Each volume in **Digital Formations** pushes forward our understanding of the intersections, and corresponding implications, between digital technologies and everyday life. The series examines broad issues in realms such as digital culture, electronic commerce, law, politics and governance, gender, the Internet, race, art, health and medicine, and education. The series emphasizes critical studies in the context of emergent and existing digital technologies.

Other recent titles include:

Felicia Wu Song
  Virtual Communities: Bowling Alone, Online Together

Edited by Sharon Kleinman
  The Culture of Efficiency: Technology in Everyday Life

Edward Lee Lamoureux, Steven L. Baron, & Claire Stewart
  Intellectual Property Law and Interactive Media: Free for a Fee

Edited by Adrienne Russell & Nabil Echchaibi
  International Blogging: Identity, Politics and Networked Publics

Edited by Don Heider
  Living Virtually: Researching New Worlds

Edited by Judith Burnett, Peter Senker & Kathy Walker
  The Myths of Technology: Innovation and Inequality

Edited by Knut Lundby
  Digital Storytelling, Mediatized Stories: Self-representations in New Media

Theresa M. Senft
  Camgirls: Celebrity and Community in the Age of Social Networks

Edited by Chris Paterson & David Domingo
  Making Online News: The Ethnography of New Media Production

To order other books in this series please contact our Customer Service Department:
  (800) 770-LANG (within the US)
  (212) 647-7706 (outside the US)
  (212) 647-7707 FAX

To find out more about the series or browse a full list of titles, please visit our website:
  WWW.PETERLANG.COM